SOUTHWEST VIRGINIA
CIVIL RIGHTS LEADER
NANNIE BERGER HAIRSTON

SOUTHWEST VIRGINIA
CIVIL RIGHTS LEADER
NANNIE BERGER HAIRSTON

AN ORAL HISTORY

SHEREE SCARBOROUGH

THE
History
PRESS

Published by The History Press
Charleston, SC
www.historypress.com

Copyright © 2025 by Sheree Scarborough

All rights reserved

First published 2025

Manufactured in the United States

ISBN 9781467153218

Library of Congress Control Number: 2024945159

Notice: The information in this book is true and complete to the best of our knowledge. It is offered without guarantee on the part of the author or The History Press. The author and The History Press disclaim all liability in connection with the use of this book.

For the children

"I want children to remember that the most important part of your life is your character. It goes with you all through your life. I learned long ago that to make it a better world, it had to begin with me."
—Nannie Berger Hairston

"WE GO ON"
(For Nannie Hairston)

We go on

Because there is this history uncelebrated…
unacknowledged…
unwanted…
That takes place each Sunday
    in church
Each Saturday
    at the juke joint
And every day of the week
When we try to make a house
A home

No one wants to understand
The faith it takes to be
A mother
A grandmother
A pillar of a distressed community

No one wants to understand
The courage it takes to be
A deacon
A janitor
A miner in the crumbling mines

Yet neither our fate
Nor our faith
Can reside in the hands
Of those who don't care
Of those who let greed be their God
Of those who tear down our meeting halls
Burn down our churches
Laugh at our steadfastness
And say "Oh, I'm sorry"
When caught in a web of lies

We go on answering
  a trumpet call
Following
  the living savior
Hoping
  for a better tomorrow

We go on because of
The strength of our soldiers
The righteousness of our battle
The need of the saved to prevail over the damned

We go on

Because we have good men and women
Good boys and girls
Good people
Who want this history
Others would destroy
To live

Nikki Giovanni, Acolytes, 2007

CONTENTS

CONTENTS

GUIDED TO A LIFE OF LEADERSHIP AND SERVICE

My Friendship with John and Nannie Hairston

I have been richly blessed by the people in my life who have helped me along the way, chief among them being Mr. John and Mrs. Nannie Hairston. My earliest recollections of them are from the days when I was a student at Friends Elementary School in Christiansburg, where their daughter Dy-Anne was one year ahead of me. I remember often seeing Mr. and Mrs. Hairston as they were together at school, church and community events. This was in the early 1960s, during the time when segregation meant that Black and White students attended different schools and segregation impacted so much of our daily life.

I remember going to movie theaters where we had to enter a side entrance and take the stairs to the balcony. I remember going to the train station and seeing the "White" and "Colored" water fountains. And then, in 1967, the schools were integrated. I am pleased to say that for the most part, in my experience, transitioning from the previously all-Black Friends Elementary to the all-White Christiansburg Elementary School was largely without incident. New friendships begun from the seventh grade and into completing Christiansburg High School were generally good. Many of the friends that I met then continue to be great friends this many years later. So, the transition, while not perfect, was relatively unremarkable. I know in other places that it wasn't as easy as what we experienced. I feel this was because of the calm and steady guidance of strong leaders in our community such as Mr. and Mrs. Hairston.

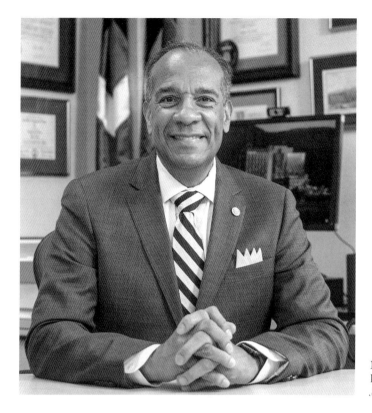

Nathaniel L.
Bishop, 2021.
Nathaniel L. Bishop.

Mr. Hairston stood out, first, because he was so tall at about six foot, five inches. His largeness was matched by the command and clarity of his voice, both the words he chose and the quality of his intonation. Mrs. Hairston, while considerably shorter standing beside her husband, was softer spoken but stood tall in her own right. Growing up, I regularly saw this influential couple, as they were actively involved and engaged in the community.

Mr. and Mrs. Hairston were friends with my parents, Reverend Elmer A. and Virginia C. Bishop, and some of their children were classmates with some of my siblings and me. My parents were also leaders in church and community life and had instilled in us values of faith in God, personal integrity, a strong work ethic and the importance of the role of service. These were values that the Hairstons also strongly embraced. My father passed away when I was fifteen years old, and as I became a young man, I was drawn to Mr. Hairston. He was a male figure who I came to deeply admire and a man who possessed qualities that I wanted to model, such as his intellect, his faith, his strength of character, his courage and his integrity.

I came into a new relationship with Mr. and Mrs. Hairston when I became an adult. It was a strict rule that adults were to be addressed as "Mr.," "Mrs." or "Miss" when I was growing up. In the transition of our relationship, while I retained high respect for both of them, it was so special to experience the evolution and melding between viewing them as adults who instructed me on what and how to do, to becoming close and personal friends. The merging of Mr. Hairston and Mrs. Hairston with John and Nan was taking place, although I never fully quite got there. Even with both giving me permission to address them by their first names, it seems the best I could do was to affectionately refer to him as "Big John," and most often I'd call her "Mamma Nan."

Our lives began to intersect much more after I became a member of the Christiansburg Police Department. After graduating high school in 1972, I attended New River Community College and had part-time jobs as a school bus driver and a gas station attendant. I was doing that while trying to discover what I really wanted to do as a career. One afternoon in the early fall of 1974, Sergeant Joe Morgan, who was a deputy sheriff with the Montgomery County Sheriff's Department, approached me at the station. Sergeant Joe had been hired as the first African American deputy sheriff. Also, over in neighboring Blacksburg, William H. (Bill) Brown had been hired as their first Black police officer in 1970. He rose through the ranks and retired as the town's storied and much-admired chief of police. Blacksburg honored him in 2022 by naming its new police department building in Chief Brown's honor.

Sergeant Morgan told me that Christiansburg was going to be annexing and expanding the size of the town. In doing so, it would need to hire four additional officers for the additional square miles that were being added. The city wanted to use the opportunity to recruit an African American to join the department. They asked him to help identify some candidates. He told me that he was there to let me know that he thought I was a good person to recommend. I was pleasantly relieved that he was not there for any official business related to me and, at the same time, shocked and surprised. As a young, somewhat radical college student, given some of the things happening at the hands of police officers at that time, becoming a police officer was not on the short list of my aspirations.

I thanked Mr. Morgan for sharing this and for his confidence in recommending me as a candidate. Over the next days, I had two voices speaking from either side of my head. On one side was a voice saying, "Look at what's happening in this country. Do you really want to become a part of this oppressive regime that seems so against young people and Black people?" On the other side, I was listening to a voice that was more akin to what I had been taught at home, in church and at school. It also spoke to some of the conversations taking place with my fellow students and close friends about the fact that our town did not have any African Americans in the police department. And this voice was saying, "Well, you can't have it both ways—you're complaining while at the same time they're offering you an opportunity. Be the change you seek. If things aren't the way you think they should be, do your part to help bring about change. You're either a part of the problem or part of the solution." The latter voice was louder and won the day. I decided to apply and accepted the offer from Chief Grover Teel, and I became Christiansburg's first African American police officer on January 1, 1975.

I was prepared by the chief and the town manager for possible negative racial reactions I might experience as I took on this new high-profile role. They told me to make them aware if anything occurred and assured me that I would have their full support. It was reassuring to hear, and I'm pleased to say that I felt they did. The same was true for the Black community. In all my relationships there, I received assurance that they were proud that I was going to be representing our community and that I had their full support. I am pleased to say that over the fourteen years I remained in the department, incidents that were of a racial nature were very few.

I will acknowledge that those first years were somewhat difficult, as I went about my work living under what I felt was the burden of tokenism. I knew that my hiring was largely driven by Christiansburg's late decision in recruiting a person of color. Even in my passion for doing a good job, the aspect of tokenism was always hanging over me. But then, after about five years, an opportunity came to apply for a promotion to an investigator position. I applied for it and got it. And not to brag or boast, I felt I was the most qualified person. That really helped change the dynamics for me. They really needed to hire me, but they didn't have to promote me. The promotion was based on merit. It helped me in working to overcome the impostor syndrome under which I had lived. It helped me to embrace more authentically what I was doing in my quest to make a difference. I liked the work I was doing, and I was good at it.

Along the way, I had discovered that I wanted to live my life and raise our family right here in Christiansburg. I was coming to this realization as I was starting to receive offers for opportunities in other places. I did not know any of my grandparents because they had passed away before I was born. My own children didn't get to meet my father, who passed before they were born, and the father of my wife, Sylvia, had passed when our two oldest were very small. I wanted my children to know and be able to love their grandmothers. I had observed that so many Black people with qualifications far greater than my own had left here and were doing some amazing things, but they were forced to pursue their careers elsewhere. There had been limited opportunities for Black people to advance in this area. I received much of my needed support and encouragement in this quandary from my conversations with John and Nan Hairston.

During those early years, they became a very important part of my support team. I enjoyed hearing them tell their own stories. I was intrigued listening to what life had been like for them in their early days in West Virginia. I enjoyed hearing about schools and education, church and community life, John's time in the military and post office and how that shaped what they brought with them when they moved to Christiansburg.

Nannie B. Hairston, John T. Hairston and Nathaniel L. Bishop, October 28, 2006. *Nathaniel L. Bishop.*

What's more, Mr. and Mrs. Hairston recognized something in me and reached out to get me more involved in the NAACP, local politics and community activities. I remember them having me over to talk about an upcoming Dr. Martin Luther King Jr. Day observance, and they said, "We want you to emcee this event." I was in my twenties, and I had always looked at older people to assume those roles. I was reluctant, but it is a scene that has played out over and over in my life: people seeing potential in me that I had not yet seen in myself. This has been so evident in my advancements from the police department to long-term healthcare administrator, to hospital administrator, to college president and to my current roles as a senior vice-president with Carilion Clinic and senior associate dean at the Virginia Tech Carilion School of Medicine. I am eternally thankful to those who saw promise in me and provided me with amazing opportunities. And in response, I have found so much joy in my life and career—in "paying it forward."

John and Nan provided opportunities like this for me. They took an interest in me, to the point that I would start going by sometimes just to talk. If John was driving by on the street, he would stop and chat. And the relationship turned from vertical to horizontal. We became friends. It was complicated, in a good way. I came to appreciate and admire him in a parent/friend combination that was just wonderful. I looked up to him, literally and figuratively. Mr. John was a strong, Black male figure in my life. I liked to tell him, "Big John, when I grow up, I want to be just like you," which always drew a fun laugh. And all the way until his health and memory declined, I continued to visit and draw on his wisdom. When he passed, I felt even more of an obligation to him. Nannie and I had been good friends but became much closer as I began looking after her and doing things I could to help her.

One of the earliest and highest awards that I have received was the 2003 Nannie B. Hairston Community Service Award. This award is presented at the annual Montgomery–Radford City–Floyd County Branch's NAACP Freedom Fund Banquet. Mrs. Hairston was awarded the Community Service Award in 1991, and thereafter, recognizing her long and dedicated commitment to principles of civil rights, social justice and equality, the award was named in her honor.

I remember working with Mrs. Hairston, Mrs. Clara Elizabeth Blake and others in the 1980s planning the annual NAACP Freedom Fund Banquet. Nan would be on the telephone contacting people, using the wealth of her connections for everything from catering to sponsorships to ticket sales. In its early days, it was held at the Christiansburg Armory. Over the years, it has grown and had to be moved to larger arenas. Prior to the 2020 pandemic, it had grown and was held at the Inn at Virginia Tech, where attendance was nearly five hundred. In the New River Valley, it had become the largest inclusive public event taking place annually, drawing a rainbow of people. Religious organizations, businesses, community service organizations, elected officials, representatives of the Democrat and Republican Parties and people of good will from all over the New River Valley came to attend this annual event.

Over the years, Mamma Nan and I had regular and many wonderful conversations. Sometimes we talked early in the morning before I went to work. We talked about family, community issues, advancing the work of programs of the NAACP and other topics of community interest. I love the fact that we had lots of laughs together as well. She told me how, in the community where she was raised, there was a Baptist church and a Methodist church, and services were held at each, on every other Sunday each month. Her family were Baptists, and like many who lived in the community, rather than miss a Sunday worship service, they attended the Methodist church on the alternate Sundays. She said that meant that she always felt as much at home in a Methodist church service as she did in a Baptist church. One of our regular laughs would come when she would preface or conclude a story with a grin and say, "You know how you Methodists are." That always brought hearty laughter and was our way of downplaying denominationalism while at the same time, speaking to the importance of being able to think and rise above difference. Mamma Nan was a master at fully embracing and owning her rich heritage and identity while acknowledging and being accepting of all others who might be different in color, religion, thought or other background.

One of my favorite memories took place during Mamma Nan's last Christmas in 2016. On Christmas Eve, I took my four granddaughters to visit with her and brought a gift. We had a great time, and I filmed as we sang Christmas carols, concluding with "Silent Night." She sang the alto part, and at the end, she looked at the girls and said, "You all didn't know that Grandma could sing, did you?" Such are my many fond memories of this "coal miner's daughter."

Two of the themes that were always present in the lessons I learned in talking with Mamma Nan were love and forgiveness. She talked about how those were needed in every family and how they, in turn, needed to be extended to all areas of our lives. In frank conversations, she would say to

N.L. Bishop with granddaughters (Sathara, Meya, Leila and Ayva) and Nannie Hairston, 2016. *Nathaniel L. Bishop.*

me, "I can talk to you like that because I knew your Mamma and Daddy." When I heard that, I knew a serious point for me to hear was about to follow. I would be sitting there, and I can still feel her put her hand on my hand or shoulder and say, "I talk to you like you're one of my own," which was a high honor. Indeed, for Nannie B. Hairston to claim me as one of her own is the very highest honor.

NATHANIEL L. BISHOP, D.MIN
Senior Vice-President and
Chief Diversity, Equity and Inclusion Officer
Carilion Clinic

Senior Associate Dean for Diversity, Inclusion
Virginia Tech Carilion School of Medicine
Roanoke, Virginia,
March 12, 2024

A NOTE ON LANGUAGE

The language we use to describe identity in this country, especially race, has evolved over time—and more than likely will keep evolving. Language is complicated and complex and powerful. Official categories of "race" change, terminologies change and cultural meanings change, as they should, because human existence is fluid and cannot be understood in strict categories. That said, I am writing this book in a cultural moment that, although challenging, is to me a time of striving for equity and inclusivity not only our language but also in the culture at large. I wish to embrace that equity and inclusivity in my writing. Therefore, I have used the *Chicago Manual of Style*'s recent decision to capitalize Black and White when referring to racial and ethnic identity as my guide. I have used this template throughout the book. And I have benefited from other authors who have recently wrestled with this issue, especially Daniel B. Thorp and Michelle J. Manno.

In addition, I have used the terms "African American," "Black" and "White" when referring to racial identity. It is important to note, however, that in the chapters of Nannie Hairston's excerpted transcripts and when I am directly quoting her, I use the words she used to describe racial and ethnic identity. She often used "Afro-American," an earlier version of "African American," and she often used "Caucasian," also an older term, rather than "White." In the same vein, she sometimes referred to enslaved individuals as "slaves." I have not changed her language to reflect the current historical moment. I felt it was important to allow her voice to speak directly to the reader.

ACKNOWLEDGEMENTS

Nannie Hairston liked to quote Hillary Clinton's well-known phrase: "It takes a village to raise a child." Indeed. I'd amend that to say it takes a village to do almost anything meaningful or long lasting. It certainly took a village to produce this book, and there are many people I need to thank. First and foremost, I am grateful to Nannie Berger Hairston, who summoned me to help tell her story and, eventually, to write her book. I am grateful to her for choosing me, for her candor, her excellent memory, her guidance, her friendship and most of all her trust in me to get the story right and true.

I am also very grateful to the Hairston family. Dy-Anne Hairston Penn opened her home to me so that I could read and scan photographs and documents from Mrs. Hairston's scrapbooks. Colette Hairston Hash has also provided many family photographs. They have also been generous in sharing information about their mother's life with me. I truly appreciate their kindness and support. Mrs. Hairston's two older daughters, Catherine and Edwina, have died since Mrs. Hairston's death in 2017.

June Stike Sayers, the former business manager at the Montgomery-Floyd Regional Library—and so much more—is next on my list of those to thank. I am forever indebted to June. She met Mrs. Hairston in 2011 after seeing an article in the *Roanoke Times* celebrating the Hairstons' seventieth wedding anniversary. She had seen Mrs. Hairston's bust in the Montgomery County Government Center many times and assumed that she had already passed—since there was a bust in the Government Center.

Mary Biggs, Nannie Hairston and June Sayers, 2013. *June Sayers.*

After she saw the article, she looked up the Hairstons' phone number and called. Mrs. Hairston invited her over. They became fast friends. June and the third-grade class of Mary W. Biggs at Harding Avenue Elementary School in Blacksburg, Virginia, nominated Mrs. Hairston for the Strong Men and Women Award in 2012, and the following year, Mrs. Hairston was awarded the honor.

June was essential to the Nannie Berger Hairston Oral History Project. Not only did she promote the need to record Nannie Hairston's life experiences with a professional oral historian, but she also sought me out according to Mrs. Hairston's wishes, introduced me to her and helped to secure the funding for the project. She has been a close advisor and supporter and has become a friend. June retired from the library in 2020, but over the last few years, she has helped me with research for this book—tirelessly and without complaint or compensation. I couldn't have done it without her.

June also recruited David Cline as an advisor to the oral history project. At the time, David was assistant professor in the Virginia Tech History

Department and today is a professor of history and the founding director of the San Diego State University Center for Public and Oral History. I thank David for his good stewardship.

I am deeply grateful to Nathaniel L. Bishop, senior vice-president and chief diversity, equity and inclusion officer at Carilion Clinic and senior associate dean for diversity and inclusion at Virginia Tech Carilion School of Medicine, who took the time out of his busy schedule to meet with me, answer myriad questions about Christiansburg, Montgomery County, segregation, integration, the workings of the NAACP and, most importantly, write the personal, heartfelt and beautiful foreword for this book.

The oral history project was fortunate to secure grant funding at the outset. I am grateful to all the granting partners: the Montgomery County Friends of the Library, the Montgomery-Floyd Regional Library Foundation, the Community Foundation of the New River Valley and the Virginia Foundation for the Humanities. I'd like to take this opportunity to also say thank you to the Montgomery-Floyd Regional Library for realizing the importance of preserving Mrs. Hairston's voice, giving me the opportunity to conduct the oral history and supporting the Nannie Hairston Oral History Project. I'm also appreciative for the opportunity to give the talk I gave about her life in 2018, "The Life and Legacy of Nannie B. Hairston." June Sayers's hand was also involved in the talk, and so thank you, June, for keeping me on track. I'd also like to thank Montgomery-Floyd Regional Library director Karim Khan as well as former director Paula K. Alston.

Montgomery County was another partner for the oral history project and supported MFRL public programming. Josh Rosenfeld filmed the video of my talk in 2018 and took fabulous photographs of the Nannie Hairston and Captain Schaeffer busts for inclusion in the book, with support from the Montgomery County Public Information Office.

There are other libraries, repositories, curators, archivists and individuals I need to thank. I am indebted to Assistant Director and Curator Sherry Joines Wyatt at the Montgomery Museum of Art & History for all her assistance in cheerfully sharing her in-depth knowledge, locating photographs and deciphering historical details. Also Jenny Nehrt, curator at the Christiansburg Institute Inc., was always helpful and responsive while providing documentary evidence and photographs that greatly enriched this book. Becky Kauffman at Craft Memorial Library in Bluefield, West Virginia, dug into the archives to locate much-needed information and photographs

Sheree Scarborough, 2018. *Sheree Scarborough.*

concerning Mrs. Hairston's West Virginia years. John M. Jackson and L.M. Rozema at the Special Collections and University Archives at Virginia Tech were also extremely helpful.

Virginia Tech history professor and author Dan Thorp shared valuable historical information with me about Montgomery County African American history; Virginia Tech philosophy professor James C. Klagge provided photographs from Freedom Fund Banquets; Bob Poff, a

Christiansburg native and past president and board member emeritus of the Montgomery Museum of Art and History, shared priceless historical details; Steven Cochran, a leader in the local, regional and state Democratic Party, provided photographs and information about the Hairstons' involvement with the Democratic Party; and Deb Travis provided much-needed help with dates and facts about the local chapter of the NAACP. I also want to thank Anne Greenwood, who as an undergraduate in the Virginia Tech History Department conducted an oral history interview with Mrs. Hairston in 2005 that was useful for me as background information. Nikki Giovanni allowed me to reprint her poem written in honor of Mrs. Hairston. Teresa Bergen carried out a masterful job on the index, a task for which I will be forever grateful. And my dear friend and oral history colleague Martha Norkunas, professor of oral and public history at Middle Tennessee State University, was an invaluable resource for scholarly advice and wisdom.

My acquisitions editor at The History Press, Kate Jenkins, has been fabulous. She has been a constant supporter and advisor for this book through many delays, pitfalls, slow starts and unending questions from me. I have very much appreciated her wise and patient counsel.

Last but not least, I am grateful to my husband, C.W. Sullivan III. Chip has not only cheered me on and supported me throughout the oral history project and the production of the book, but being an English professor, he is also an excellent editor, and I have called on his skills. His skills are not confined to the editor's desk, however. He is an excellent chef and sommelier, and those skills helped me survive.

INTRODUCTION

I'm not telling something to make it sound good. I'm just telling the way it was.
—Nannie Berger Hairston

I magine this story, if you will: You are born Black and female in Deep Appalachia in the American South in the early twentieth century, just fifty-some odd years beyond the end of the Civil War and slavery. You move from town to town because your father is a coal miner and worked in mines without unions. You are bused to a segregated one-room schoolhouse, where you had to wait in the cold coming and going. You live through the Great Depression. You graduate from high school, marry and start raising your children. Your husband is a coal miner and loses his job, so you move to another area in the South and know no one. The area is very restrictive: You can't eat in most of the restaurants, you can't go to the movies, your children are sent to a segregated school with old textbooks and you only have the lowest paid jobs available to you—you know your place. And yet because of your background and how you were taught to love, not hate, and get involved and give back to your community, you become a leader and pillar of that community. You advocate for change and civil rights and opportunities for all. You raise a family who also grow up to fight for civil rights and social justice. You have a bust carved in your likeness and placed in the county's government center. You become friends with mayors and senators, visit the White House and receive letters from governors and even presidents. You become an icon, sought after for your advice and beloved by

Blacks and Whites, young and old, Democrats and Republicans, men and women, preachers and sinners, officeholders and newcomers, rich and poor. Your voice is the voice for love—a voice this country so desperately needs right now. This is the story of Nannie Berger Hairston.

I CONDUCTED A SERIES of oral history interviews with Nannie Hairston in 2015–16. In the afterword, I describe the process in detail. This introduction sets her story in time and place, as do the prefaces that accompany each chapter. The chapters themselves are in her words. I have also shared a few of her most powerful and evocative quotations in the introduction in order to introduce the reader to her remarkable story and to her wit, commonsense and wisdom.

Nannie Hairston liked to call herself a "coal miner's daughter," with a nod to Loretta Lynn's classic country song. And she was. She was born in 1921 in Bottom Creek, West Virginia, which is an unincorporated community in McDowell County. McDowell County, in the very southern part of the state and situated in the rich Pocahontas Field, was the epicenter of the coal mining industry in the twentieth century. In the 1920s in McDowell County, there were 86,345 Black people in a total population of 1,463, 701. But in 1950, there were only approximately 25,000 African Americans and 100,000 residents in the county, just before Nannie and her family left.[1] As a sad aside, in the 2020 census, the county's total population was under 20,000, was the third-poorest county in the country and was suffering from high rates of deaths from drug overdoses and low levels of life expectancy.[2]

The rise of the coal industry in West Virginia, especially in the southern counties such as McDowell County, had been steep. At the end of the Civil War, there was no commercial coal mining, but by 1920, a year before Nannie's birth, the state was the second-largest producer of coal in the nation just under Pennsylvania.[3] Coal operators and companies with their company towns, expanding railroads and influx of European immigrants and African Americans from the southern states to work in the mines—part of a first wave of the Great Migration—radically changed the physical and social landscape of the state. These coal mines were also a very dangerous place to work. In the first three decades of the twentieth century, coal miner deaths in the region were the highest of any coal producing state.[4]

McDowell County became the major region in the state for African American miners and their families, with the concomitant development of community and its separate Black churches, fraternal organizations, mutual

Above: Nannie Hairston,
2010. *Hairston family*.

Right: Nannie Mae Berger,
1922. *Hairston family*.

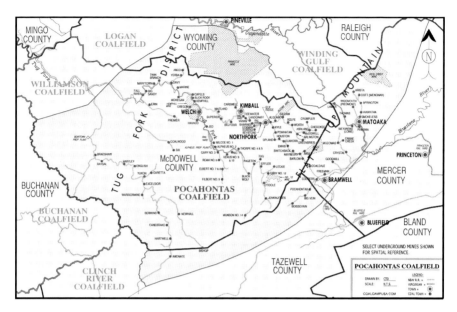

Flat Top–Pocahontas coal field map. *Coalcampusa.com.*

aid societies and schools. By 1931, African Americans made up 34 percent of all coal miners in McDowell County.[5]

Southern West Virginia is also known for its history of labor strikes, known as the West Virginia Coal Wars, many of which turned violent when the United Mine Workers of America (UMWA) was working to unionize the industry because of the unsafe and deplorable conditions, but the coal companies backed by the state government resisted. The Paint Creek Mine War in Kanawha County (1912–13), in which at least fifty lost their lives to violence and many more to starvation, received national attention when labor organizer Mary Harris "Mother" Jones was jailed for her role. The Battle of Matewan of Mingo County in 1920 was a shootout between miners and the Baldwin-Felts Detective Agency, which had been hired by the Stone Mountain Coal Company.[6] Most famous and most violent was the Battle of Blair Mountain—the largest labor uprising in American history. For five days from late August to September 1921—just after Nannie Berger was born and only seventy-five miles to the north of her birthplace—ten thousand armed coal miners confronted three thousand lawmen and strike breakers when the miners were trying to unionize. The conflict ended when President Warren Harding sent in the U.S. Army. It is estimated that one hundred miners died and almost one thousand were arrested.[7] In the Battle of Blair Mountain, Black and White miners fought together to unionize, and numerous Black miners died.[8]

This was the background into which Nannie Berger Hairston was born. Nannie's father, Samuel Berger, worked in non-union mines in West Virginia during Nannie's childhood. Her family lived in small towns (Bottom Creek, Crumpler, English, Excelsior and Faraday) throughout McDowell County because the small mines Mr. Berger worked for would close or fire their workers on short notice from time to time. He joined the union while employed at Pocahontas Fuel Company in the late 1930s after the federal government under President Franklin Delano Roosevelt enacted legislation that guaranteed trade union rights under the National Industrial Recovery Act in 1933, and Congress passed the National Labor Relations Act in 1935. After Mr. Berger joined the union, the family didn't move again until they left the state for Virginia in 1953.

"Everywhere We Ever Lived, [My Father] Made a Garden on the Mountainside"

Although they moved often and it was a hardscrabble existence—Nannie was ten years old in 1931 so her teenage years were during the Great Depression—she had fond memories of her childhood. Her family was close-knit. She lovingly remembers her father's garden. She told stories about childhood pranks with her siblings—she was the eldest of ten—and recounted stories of playing croquet, baseball and basketball, shooting marbles and roller-skating in the neighborhood. And she would dream.

"I'm On My Way to Washington, to the White House"

"I think I told you the story when I was young, I used to sit in the swing. On our front porch, the swing went this way, and the steps were there where you walk up on the front porch. You went on the front porch as you come out the door and walked that way. I would be sitting in the swing, and when the engineer on the train who was coming to get the coal to take it to whatever state they going to sell it to, I would be swinging, and the engineer would honk the horn on the engine. We were that close to the railroad. But they could see me, and he would honk then, pull it down. And I always said to myself, 'I'm on my way to Washington, to the White House.'" (January 19, 2016)

However, the underside of that story, growing up in the time of Jim Crow in the American South—when state and local laws enforced racial segregation—was always present. She talked about her segregated schools, segregated baseball fields, segregated cinema and the tennis courts where Black citizens couldn't play at all.

West Virginia has a complicated history when it comes to Jim Crow. Although there were no Black codes in West Virginia—the precursor to Jim Crow laws—the social and legal systems of racism that mandated segregated public facilities, transportation and education existed and were enforced. And the threat of violence was as present as it was across the South during this time for those who dared to challenge the system. There were fewer lynchings in the state than any other state in the South—by some estimates fifty occurred between 1882 and 1968.[9] In addition, West Virginia passed the Capehart Anti-Lynching Law in 1921, the same year that Nannie was born. Even so, in 1931 a high-profile lynching of two African Americans occurred in Greenbrier County, which was about one hundred miles from McDowell County. And the 1910s and early 1920s saw a resurgence of the Ku Klux Klan in all parts of the country, including McDowell County, West Virginia. Enough cannot be said for the strong foundation of growing up in a loving home that taught love instead of hate, even while being surrounded by so much hate.

"We Just Knew Our Place"

"We couldn't go in hotels and sleep. We couldn't go in to eat in the restaurant that would serve you. You knew you couldn't sit down. You could go in and buy and come out. But some wouldn't even sell to you. That's the way I look at life. If you haven't been taught to love instead of hate, you would have a miserable life going through the world hating people for what they have done and done to your grandparents and your great-grands. But I happened to be fortunate enough to have parents that didn't carry that hate. What was passed on to us has been a beautiful life for me and my children." (August 25, 2015)

Her parents, her relatives, the African American community and most especially the schools and the church provided stability and safety, as they did in many such communities across the country.

One of the constant threads in the interviews is the importance of her mother, Bessie, in her life. Her father, Samuel, was important to her as well,

Bessie Mae Berger
on her ninety-
sixth birthday,
Christiansburg,
Virginia, 1996.
Hairston family.

but she called her mother her "role model." This corresponds with many oral histories of African American women from Nannie's generation who have spoken of their mothers as "heroes."[10] In Nannie's case, her mother modeled behaviors to her daughter that later became central to her life and her life's work.

In later years, Nannie Hairston was a fierce advocate for the right to vote and the importance of voting and was a founding member of the local League of Women Voters. She remembers the fact that her mother voted for Franklin Delano Roosevelt for president.

> *"Because years ago, all colored people were thinking that they had to vote Republican because of Abraham Lincoln. That was the big deal until they really found out. And these are the words I heard my mother say. That's why I can remember Mr. Roosevelt. She told my aunt, she said, 'Irene, I'm going to change my vote. It can't get any worse. I'm going to vote for Mr. Roosevelt.' And she did." (December 1, 2015)*

Hairston family (Fred Miles with Monica and baby Melissa, Nannie, John, Colette, Edwina Hairston Miles and Dy-Anne) in Washington, D.C., 1969. *Hairston family.*

In fact, voting was important to both her mother and father. Even though her mother had a fourth-grade education and her father had no formal education, her parents voted in every election. And because their education had been truncated, they believed strongly in education for their children. Education—and equality in education—became one of Nannie Hairston's major focuses later in life: education for her children, for the children of her community, for college students who had no place to stay on the nearby university campus, for college students who couldn't afford the next semester's study and for children who needed a place for a preschool or after school lessons in Black history.

In addition, Nannie Hairston was her own archivist, collecting African American history from and for her community. She also collected more general tracts, such as a booklet listing inventions by Black inventors, and she shared this knowledge with others. When we met, she had a large collection of scrapbooks that included photographs, brochures, letters, newspaper articles, journal entries, lists and handwritten cards.

Once her father was in the union, the Berger family stayed put in Faraday, West Virginia. But Nannie went to the same school from elementary to high school in Excelsior, West Virginia, because that was the only school for African Americans in the vicinity. She and her younger siblings were bused fifteen miles each way. The bus picked up the African American children first at about 7:00 a.m. and took them home last at the end of the day. Well, Mrs. Hairston's mother changed that when her younger children were in elementary school.

"MY MOTHER WAS A ROSA PARKS"

"It was when her smaller children were in grade school and had to ride the same bus. They would have to go and wait until the teacher came in at eight o'clock. That's about two hours and something, waiting in the cold.…She said, 'I'm tired,' and she pawned her sewing machine to Mr. Jesse Pew. I'll never forget him. He had a car with a thing called a rumble seat in the back. He picked the sewing machine up with another man helping him, and put it in his car, and let my mother have $5 to pay somebody to carry her to the school board to make her complaint.…She went by herself.…And, from what I have heard, the time frame was about a month. Somebody said, 'Mama, there goes a McDowell County truck with lumber on it.' That's when they started hauling the lumber to get ready to build a [Black] school, right there in Faraday, West Virginia." *(August 25, 2015)*

Nannie Hairston was greatly influenced by her mother's political activism, and it pointed the way years later when she got heavily involved in the National Association for the Advancement of Colored People (NAACP), the Democratic Party, the Parent Teacher Association (PTA) and many other organizations to make a difference in the lives of her community.

Nannie attended Excelsior High School, which was located in War, West Virginia, about ten miles from her home in Faraday. Excelsior, opened in 1923, was one of thirty-eight all-Black schools in the state. It has been described as having a beautiful campus with a red brick building and manicured lawn. It also had highly qualified teachers with bachelor's and master's degrees. She graduated in 1939, one of nineteen graduates—one of whom was her future husband, John Tyrone Hairston—with a class motto of "Knowledge is Power." She and John were both inducted in the West Virginia All Black Schools Sports and Academic Hall of Fame in 2008.[11]

A pivotal moment for Nannie was when the church's missionary society helped her buy her senior ring, which was $9.50 in 1939. This was during the Depression, and her family could not afford to buy it. Her mother's "missionary work" or volunteer work influenced the life's work of Nannie Hairston. Bessie Berger was very involved in the church's women's missionary society. Nannie vowed to help make a difference in others' lives at that point. She made good on her vow. She became a leader in her church, a deaconess and a member of the Order of the Eastern Star and also helped people outside her role of volunteering for these organizations.

"You Can't Fight Hate with Nothing but Love"

Nannie married her high school classmate John Hairston in 1941 and moved to Faraday, West Virginia, three miles from her home in Amonate. In 1945, John was drafted into the army during World War II and served in postwar cleanup operations. He returned home the following year, stayed in the Army Reserves, was recalled to active duty during the Korean War and served until 1952, when he was wounded and honorably discharged. John was a decorated veteran: he received the Purple Heart and Silver Star, as well as other awards for his service. Just a short time after he had returned from Korea, after he began to work in the coal mines again, the mine abruptly closed in 1953.

John heard that they were hiring at the Radford Army Ammunition Plant in Christiansburg, Virginia, about one hundred miles to the east of Amonate, and immediately found a job there. He also got a job for his father-in-law, who had lost his job in the mine as well. So Nannie and John packed up their two young daughters and her parents and moved to Christiansburg. They found a place on a hill rich in African American history with just under ten acres. They lived there the rest their lives.

This is where they raised their family of four daughters. Nannie's parents lived with them for a few years until they could build their own home nearby, and other family members lived there with them from time to time, as did some of their children's friends who needed a warm, loving home.

Right: John Hairston, World War II. *Hairston family*.

Below: Hairston home, Christiansburg, Virginia. *Hairston family*.

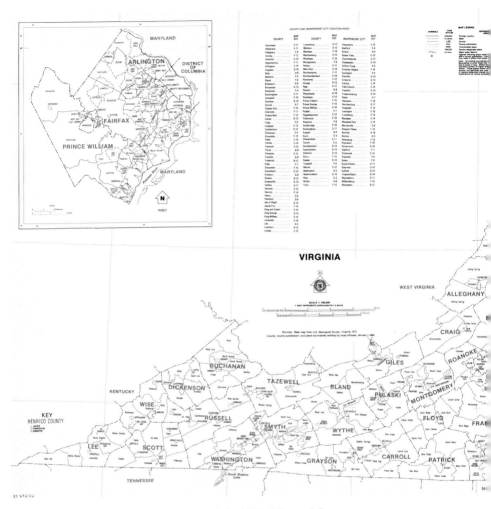

Base map from U.S. Geological Survey, Virginia, 1973. *Library of Congress.*

Christiansburg, Virginia, in 1953 had a population of about 3,000, with 5 percent African Americans (that would have been 150 to 200 people). Christiansburg is the county seat of Montgomery County, a mostly rural county—especially so in the 1950s—in the southwestern part of the state and the eastern edge of Appalachia. It sits at the crossroads of three major highways: U.S. Route 11, U.S. Route 460 and I-81. In addition, the Norfolk & Western Railroad had a popular depot in Christiansburg. It is only a few miles south of Blacksburg, where Virginia Tech is located.

"ALWAYS REMEMBER THIS:
WHERE YOU COULD GO, I COULDN'T"

In the 1950s and early 1960s, Christiansburg was a segregated community dominated by Jim Crow. This would not have been too different from the coal fields of West Virginia, except that the Pocahontas Fuel Company, where Nannie's father ended up working and her husband worked, was integrated to a certain degree. Black and White workers could shop in the same company store and lived on the same street (albeit on opposite sides of the street). And, of course, Black and White men worked in the mines together.

There were also differences in degree between West Virginia and Virginia in terms of the history of racism, Jim Crow laws and violence against African Americans. Whereas West Virginia did not have Black codes that were established during Reconstruction to racially segregate and restrict the lives of African Americans, Virginia did have such codes. The Ku Klux Klan saw a resurgence in the 1920s in Virginia, along with the rest of the nation. Virginia did pass an anti-lynching law in 1928, called one of the most stringent in the country, as there had been several high-profile lynchings that caused national outrage.[12] Klan activity died down some after that time. The Klan resurfaced in the 1950s and 1960s to oppose the civil rights movement nationwide and in Virginia, about the time the Hairstons arrived in the state. There were purportedly one hundred lynchings in the state of Virginia— twice that of West Virginia—between 1882 and 1968.[13]

But there were some major advantages for African Americans in Christiansburg. There was a vibrant downtown area with thriving Black businesses—restaurants, a hotel included in the *The Negro Motorist Green Book* and a Black-owned cab company. The Christiansburg Institute was also located there, with its rich history as the only educational institution for African Americans in Southwest Virginia, serving up to fifteen surrounding counties. It was founded in 1866 by Captain Charles S. Schaeffer, was led for a period of time in the early 1900s by Booker T. Washington and in 1947 was deeded to local school districts. Christiansburg Institute plays a large role in Nannie Hairston's life and will be explored in greater detail in the chapters to come.

View east along West Main Street from Hickok Street, circa 1960. *D.D. Lester Collection, Montgomery Museum.*

Aerial, Christiansburg Institute, 1963. *D.D. Lester Collection, Montgomery Museum.*

The Hairstons established themselves in the community. One of their first acts upon moving to Christiansburg was to join the Schaeffer Memorial Baptist Church. They both became very involved and stayed involved all their lives. Nannie told me that she joined the church before John, shortly after arriving in Christiansburg, just a month or two before their third daughter was born, when mother and baby had to stay in the crowded, segregated ward of the local hospital. John joined the NAACP before she did. But they joined each other in those organizations soon thereafter—a metaphor for their life together.

Nannie Hairston held numerous jobs over the years—jobs that were available to her as an African American woman. She briefly worked as a maid making fifty cents per hour, she worked as an insurance agent selling insurance to other African Americans, she was a seamstress in the local garment factory (the Christiansburg Garment Company) and finally worked at the Radford Army Ammunition Plant, where she rose through the ranks, was a member of the union and retired in 1983 after twenty years.

"Do You Want to Help Yourself for Tomorrow or Just for Today?"

One story from her time working in the garment factory exemplifies Nannie Hairston's courage and belief in making the world a better place and her push for civil rights. She approached the Christiansburg Garment Company once or twice to inquire about a position and in the end brought several African American women friends with her. They all got jobs. And although they worked in the same large room with all the White women workers, their stations were in a corner of the room together. And when it came time for the yearly picnic, the manager, William Phillips, came to Nannie and told her that she and her friends wouldn't be invited, but he was willing to give them money so that they could have their own picnic.[14] Although the other African American women wanted to take Mr. Phillips's money, she advised them not to: "Think about it. Do you want to help yourself for tomorrow or just for today?" They decided not to take the money, and the next year, the policy changed so that the all could attend the picnic.

Christiansburg Blouse Factory, April 1965. *Montgomery Museum.*

Hairston family at Christmastime. *Hairston family.*

In 1954, one year after the Hairstons moved to Christiansburg, the landmark *Brown v. Board of Education* ruling that outlawed segregated education in America was passed by the Supreme Court. However, Virginia—led by Republican senator Harry F. Byrd—mounted a strategy called massive resistance that delayed the integration of schools. Several school districts across the state shut down rather than integrate. Lawsuits went on for years by segregationists attempting to prevent integration and by the NAACP to force the state to abide by the Supreme Court's *Brown* ruling. It wasn't until another Supreme Court ruling, *Green v. County School Board of New Kent County* in 1968, that the strategies employed by massive resistance were declared unconstitutional.

The schools did not shut down in Christiansburg, but they didn't integrate until the school year of 1966–67. Nannie Hairston, as you might expect, was involved with the PTA when her daughters were in school. Her two older daughters, Catherine and Edwina, attended the newly built segregated Friends Elementary School when it opened in September 1953.[15] The school was built at the behest of Black parents because of overcrowding at the Hill School, part of the Christiansburg Institute. And when African Americans were admitted to Virginia Tech in the 1950s but denied housing until 1961, the Hairstons provided a place to stay until a long-term solution for the students could be found.[16] "We were just like a hotel reception," she said.

The Hairstons became leaders in the African American community, and their home was an informal meeting place for young African Americans trying to make their way in the world. Later in the 1980s and 1990s and beyond, their home would become a meeting place for advice seekers of all colors, political parties, persuasions, genders and ages.

"WHEREVER YOU MOVE, BE A PART OF THE COMMUNITY"

The Hairstons served on many boards and were active members in numerous organizations. They got involved. As Mrs. Hairston said many times, her parents taught her, "Wherever you move, be a part of your community." Nannie Hairston was involved in the Virginia Council on Human Relations; Montgomery County League of Women Voters, of which she was a founding member; the local chapter of the United Way, of which she was the first African American member; the Christiansburg Community Center Board, which, in part, oversees the Hill School (the original site of the Christiansburg Institute that she championed all her life); the NAACP; and the Democratic Party.

The Hairstons especially made their mark on the local NAACP branch. The 1950s and 1960s were a difficult time, as the civil rights movement was beginning to be felt with marches and sit-ins across the South, Supreme Court cases challenging the status quo and the assassinations of leaders of the movement and politicians. Even in the 1980s, the Ku Klux Klan (KKK) was marching. John was president of the local chapter of the NAACP in the 1980s, and Nannie served as treasurer, membership chair and co-advisor for the Youth Council over the years. They were lifetime members and received many awards from the organization over the years.

Nannie Hairston, November 1974. *Hairston family.*

"AND THEY HAVEN'T BEEN BACK IN MONTGOMERY COUNTY TO MARCH SINCE"

One of the stories she told me was the time that the KKK planned to march in Christiansburg in 1986.

> *"Yes, and they were going to march. And by the time we got where they were going to march, it was just as pretty as that light sunshine, as that light is shining over there. And by the time they got on Roanoke Street and lined up to march, a clap of thunder came. Then all at once, sweetheart, it just started raining, and everybody ran and got into their car and that was the end of that. It just doesn't seem real. But that's what happened, right here on Roanoke Street. And they haven't been back in Montgomery County to march since." (December 1, 2015)*

One of the Hairstons' most important legacies is the NAACP Annual Freedom Fund Banquet. Nannie was rightfully very proud of its popularity and the fact that people from all walks of life attended. I was fortunate to be able to sit at her table for several years.

Freedom Fund Banquet, October 2016. *Sheree Scarborough.*

"Don't Ever Let Anyone Tell You One Vote Doesn't Matter. It Does."

The Hairstons also both served in the local Democratic Party and worked countless hours for national, state and local candidates. One such candidate was Madison Marye, who served in the Virginia Senate from 1973 to 2002. A story that Mrs. Hairston shared with me was one that shows how long de facto segregation stayed on in some areas of the South. She told me about her youngest daughter, who was with her while she was campaigning for Senator Marye in the fall of 1972. It was cold and it was raining, and they had been out all week. Colette was hungry. She took Colette into a restaurant and was told by the proprietor, "You know we can't serve you." But it was almost closing time, and they were ushered into the "other side" of the restaurant, where they couldn't be seen and ate their soup. This was in 1972.

Later, the Maryes became friends with the Hairstons, and Madison wrote her a poignant letter when she was invited to the White House by President

Dear ~~Fellow Democrat,~~ *Nannie*

As our time in the White House draws to a close, we want to take a moment to thank you.

Looking back at the past eight years, we are overwhelmingly grateful for the unwavering support you've given our family. Your devotion to our country – and to the Democratic Party – has made all the difference in our work to change America for the better.

Thanks to your commitment, 20 million more Americans have access to quality health care, marriage equality is the law of the land, our businesses have created millions of new jobs, and we have taken historic steps to combat climate change. And in the years ahead, we'll have to keep up that work – together – not only to protect the progress we made, but to advance the causes of opportunity and justice for every single American.

You've always fueled our faith in the future. Even when the odds were overwhelming. Even when the road ahead was long. You kept us going. We hope we did the same for you.

So please accept our heartfelt gratitude for everything you've done. Your loyalty has meant so much to us and the Democratic Party, and it means so much for the future of our country. Let's keep fighting to move our country forward.

Gratefully,

Barack *Michelle*

Barack and Michelle Obama

Nannie, we'll never forget the support you've given us. Thank you and Happy Holidays!

Letter from Barack and Michelle Obama. *Hairston family.*

Jimmy Carter in 1980 that included these lines: "Nan, I'm sitting down here in Richmond, I can think of no other person in the area who has been invited to the White House. I've been in Montgomery County all my life, and I can't think of anyone to get a invitation." Mrs. Hairston said to me, "He didn't mention a president of the men's club or some organization that's outstanding in the county. He said, 'I can't think of any [other] person to get an invitation to the White House.' He didn't identify me as Black, just Nan. And that's something."

So, that little girl sitting on the porch swing in West Virginia who became the woman Nannie Berger Hairston did go to the White House. And more than that, she knew and advised mayors, governors, senators, congressmen and presidential candidates and drew accolades from all of the above and even from sitting presidents.

"IF YOU CAN'T DO IT OUT OF LOVE YOU NEED TO STOP. THAT'S MY MOTTO."

The legacy that Nan and John Hairston left their community is one of accomplishing things for the good and making the community a better place. Their voices—her voice—became synonymous with social justice for African Americans, yes, but also for anyone who needed help in the community. And they worked with others to ensure that fighting for that equality and justice was done without violence.

> *"I try to tell people now sometimes you've got to have a way of knowing how to address yourself to people to get something done. A lot of us now, we see the newspaper, it looks like the violence is—we aren't teaching how not to have it. We're just going in, it doesn't matter—just everybody on that side of the fence and on this side of the fence." (December 1, 2015)*

John and Nannie Hairston spent their lives reaching across that fence. John died in 2012, and Nannie died in 2017. They were married seventy years and had four loving daughters, and at the time of her death, Nannie Hairston had nine grandchildren and eleven great-grandchildren. There was a community-wide outpouring of grief and lauding of accomplishments when she died. She was revered.

Both John and Nannie Hairston received many awards during their lifetimes. Nannie received the Strong Men and Women in Virginia History

Clockwise, from top left: John and Nannie Hairston at Martin Luther King Jr. grave site. *Hairston family*; Nannie and John Hairston, John's seventy-fifth birthday, June 1995. *Hairston family*; Nannie Berger Hairston bust, Montgomery County Government Center, 2023. *Josh Rosenfeld*; Nannie B. Hairston, 2013. *From the* Roanoke Tribune.

Award from the Library of Virginia and Dominion Energy in 2013 (the award's inaugural year) and a NAACP award in her honor, to name only two of her honors. She is commemorated with a bronze bust in the Montgomery County Government Center, the Virginia House of Delegates issued proclamations honoring both Nannie and John after their deaths and there is a John T. and Nannie B. Hairston Day (June 14) in Christiansburg.

But more than her legacy in Christiansburg, Virginia, Montgomery County—and even Southwest Virginia—Nannie Hairston leaves a legacy to the United States of America and the values on which it was founded. She was one of the many activists across the country who believed in the ideals of equality, liberty and justice for all. She worked most of her life to help form a more perfect union—believed in it, had faith in it and passed that belief and faith down to successive generations. She and her husband, John, worked quietly behind the scenes, sat through hundreds of hours of meetings, helped raise money for worthy causes, mentored and tutored, licked thousands of envelopes, gave speeches, voted, took people to vote and spoke to business owners, mayors, senators and governors. In the history of the civil rights movement behind (and in front of) its important leaders—Martin Luther King Jr., Rosa Parks, Jesse Jackson, Andrew Young, Julian Bond and John Lewis—there was an army of African Americans (and yes, some Whites) who believed in the promise of what America could be and helped to further it along its way. Nannie Berger Hairston was one of these brave, resilient and remarkable individuals, and she did it out of love. Listen as she tells her story.

> *"I'm just thinking how we have gone through so much, because our family back in 1619 came here from Africa. We got here before the people from Europe got here, 1620 to 1621. We were already here, and we tilled the soil, built America, and we still—it's almost like you hear the president say, 'No child left behind.' I say, 'No race left behind.' We're still trying to pull ourselves up with our bootstraps to make us to be what we want to be as citizens in America." (December 16, 2015)*

HER STORY

Chapter 1

WEST VIRGINIA CHILDHOOD, 1921–1941

"I had a beautiful life of being poor."

A STRONG FOUNDATION

Nannie Mae Berger was born on August 7, 1921, in Bottom Creek, a small town in McDowell County, West Virginia. She was the eldest child of Samuel Berger and Bessie Mae Robinson Berger, who would go on to have ten children (Nannie Mae, Blanche Louise, Rosa Lee, Catherine, Samuel Jr., Henry Dean, Janella, Arlene Francis, Shirley Anita and Maxine). The family moved frequently, as they followed coal mining jobs before the formation of unions in rural West Virginia: Crumpler, English, Excelsior and finally Faraday, all within McDowell County.

It was a challenging existence, as the family had to battle racism, the inequality and segregation of Jim Crow and the Great Depression. In these small towns, Nannie went to one-room schoolhouses that were lacking in materials, basic necessities and even heat. She and her brothers and sisters were bused many miles to attend these segregated schools until her mother took a stand to request that a closer school be built to their community—and it was. Education for their children was important to her parents, as her mother had a fourth-grade education and her father did not have the opportunity to attend school. All of their children graduated from high school, and two of their daughters, Rosa and Arlene, went to college.

Nannie talks about the resilience of her parents and the dedication with which they raised their children. Her father always had a garden, her mother canned and they raised chickens and hogs. She recounted stories of typical childhood games that she and her siblings played—jacks, baseball, circle games, roller-skating and even croquet. But she also remembered not being able to play tennis, go swimming or play softball until a special recreation area was built for African Americans. Everywhere there was the specter of race. However, she remembers the love with which her parents surrounded her and her brothers and sisters. They were taught to love, not hate.

The family attended Lily of the Valley Baptist Church, but the congregation shared the building with a Methodist church on alternate Sundays. Her mother was a midwife and was called on by the local White doctors to help with births, and in fact, before her marriage, she had been a caregiver for African Americans who had tuberculosis before there was a segregated sanatorium where they could be treated. After her mother's marriage, Bessie Mae Berger was very active in the church's missionary society. Although she had been pulled out of school in the fourth grade to take care of her siblings when her mother died, she was a reader who read a wide array of publications, including newspapers, magazines, books and the Bible. She shared her life philosophy liberally with her children: respect others; work hard, save and elevate yourself; and most importantly, love is the only thing that can fight hate. Her mother, as Nannie Berger Hairston told me many times, was her role model.

Nannie's father was also a large influence on her life, albeit a quieter one. She didn't know much about her father's family, but she always tried to learn about the Bergers. She did know that her grandparents Annie Mariah Berger and Peyton Berger were landowners and farmers in Franklin County, Virginia. They had died by the time her father was sixteen years old. Her father worked on the family farm, trained horses and, interestingly, worked for a while in Christiansburg, Virginia, for the Childress family before moving on to the mines in West Virginia. Samuel Berger was a gentle, compassionate man who cooked, nursed, farmed and gardened—in addition to working in the mines—to help provide for his family. He had no formal education but was adept at numbers and passed on to his children the importance of common sense.

In 1939, Nannie graduated from Excelsior Negro High School. A few years before that, unions came to the coal mines, and her father joined. So the family was able to stay put in Faraday, West Virginia, where her father worked for Pocahontas Fuel Company. Nannie has fond memories of Faraday and also of Amonate, Virginia. The small towns were three miles apart. She remembers that the Pocahontas Fuel Company store and

Excelsior Negro High School Choir, Excelsior, West Virginia, circa 1938–39. *Hairston family*.

restaurant were integrated, the recreation areas in the towns were large and included a space for African Americans to play sports and there was a cinema with a segregated seating area.

Nannie moved the three miles to Amonate when she married her high school classmate John Tyrone Hairston in 1941. John had been on the track team and was captain of the football team, and in fact, he had been selected for the West Virginia All-State Football Team for Negro High Schools in 1937. She and John were both members of the Excelsior Negro High School Choir. Nannie was also athletic and played on a women's baseball team, the Faraday Yellow Jackets, established by Pocahontas Fuel Company, before her marriage. She played shortstop. John also played baseball for the Pocahontas Fuel Company after high school while he worked for the mine. John and Nannie didn't date in high school, but after John went to the World's Fair in California in 1939, he came by her house to share what he learned. It was the beginning of a partnership with profound consequences not only for themselves and their family but also for the communities in which they found themselves.

ANCESTORS

"You can't fight hate with nothing but love."

Millers

The only story I ever heard of slavery was my mother's grandmother. They didn't call them maids; they called them house slaves. She was there whenever the master didn't want to go to bed with his wife. Her mother's mother was named Liza. Well, when something happened, I guess she didn't produce as he wanted, so he sold her. When he sold her to another slave owner, he put her in the tobacco field, and she didn't know how to work. And by her not working like they wanted her to—because she didn't know how—he hit her in the back of the neck with a tobacco stick. Mama said when slavery was over, she was like this all her life, sitting in the corner, because she never had any help. Her neck was just bent over, and she was shaking until she died. That's the only thing that I ever heard of any [slavery in the family]. Of course, that would have been my great-great-grandmother. It's a sad story, but it's a true story.

My mother's motto with her family was: "You can't fight hate with nothing but love." That's the way I look at life. If you haven't been taught to love instead of hate, you would have a miserable life going through the world

West Virginia Colored Orphans Home, *West Virginia and Regional History Center, West Virginia University Libraries.*

Girls, Colored Orphans Home, 1912. *West Virginia and Regional History Center, West Virginia University Libraries.*

hating people for what they have done to your grandparents and your great-grands and your uncles and great-uncles. But I happened to be fortunate enough to have parents that didn't carry that hate. What was passed on to us has been a beautiful life for me, and friends, and my children.

My mother's mother [Liza Miller Robinson] died when my mother was eight years old. Well, I don't know how long it was before they had taken them away, but it had to have been within a month or so, in the early part of the year after Grandma died. They carried them to Huntington, West Virginia, to a children's home. My mother said they had certain times they had to go to bed. That's why when she raised us, when we went to bed, my mother said, "You're not supposed to disturb the other people over in the other room." She was taught that in that home. They must have been there about a year or so before my granddaddy [Henry Robinson] could get them out, but he got them.

This is a story my mother used to tell me, or not just me, but would tell and I would hear over and over whenever she [told it]. Her brother was the youngest, and Aunt Marie was next. Aunt Marie and then Aunt Mary and Ike. His name was Isaac, but they called him Ike. They were going to separate them. Mama said the matron of the place knew my mother was close to her brother and her two sisters. She said, "She told us, 'You just go in there and cry and just holler, just as loud as you can cry, and maybe we can save your sisters and them from being taken away from you, you all being separated.'" Wasn't that something? And she did that and it worked.

My father's mother and father died before he was sixteen years old. So I only had one grandparent growing up in my life, which, with ten children in the family, we never knew—actually, after me, none of the children had grandparents, because my mother's father died when I was eleven years old.

Bergers

The most important thing about my father's life that I could tell you is when my father was twenty-five years old he married my mother at seventeen years old. And my grandfather almost disapproved, I would say, of my father marrying my mother, because my mother was taken out of school in the fourth grade to take care of the rest of the family. And at this point I think my grandfather was thinking that he was losing everything that he had.

But the most beautiful part of it—my grandfather got injured in the mines and couldn't work anymore. My father asked my grandfather with three children to come and live with him and my mother, and they all grew up with us. That's why I had an uncle and two aunts, and I always called them by their name. And everyone couldn't figure out, "Why don't you say 'Aunt'?" But they were so close to me, playing with me, as they were growing.

My grandfather lived with my daddy and mother until he died. Those three children, a son and two daughters, lived with my father and mother as their children. So we started out in life with a family sharing with each other. That's why my life has been so beautiful. It isn't something that I had to make myself want to take care of you. It's automatically in my life to feel that towards anyone, because my parents just shared all their life with people.

[In addition to being a coal miner] my daddy was a horse trainer. I can't tell you how he learned it, when he learned it, but that's the kind of person my father was. And he used to trade horses. Some [people] just weren't used to a Black man, a colored man, riding horses and having a good horse. You see what I'm saying?

This is not such a good story. He had gotten his foot hurt in the mines. Coal or slate, something fell on it, and he couldn't work. He had riding horses, and he rode his horse over to the stock market, where they were trading horses. And this White man wanted my father to trade the horse he was riding, and he told him no, and almost created a fight right there. I don't know if he hit my daddy first or my daddy hit him first. I think Daddy probably hit him first because somehow or another my daddy's foot hit something. I don't know what happened. But the policeman of that town—not the policeman of the state, but of that town, Crumpler, [West Virginia]—told my father, "You all go home." He told that to all the colored men that were there trading horses. They wanted my daddy to trade, and he wouldn't. So he told them, "Go home. When it gets dark, cut the lights out. Get your guns ready because when they find out where you live, they may come and make you trade horses or shoot your family or whatever." But they never did come.

COAL MINER'S DAUGHTER

"Everywhere we ever lived, he made a garden on the mountainside."

Whenever we'd see Mama and Daddy killing chickens and Mama frying them up, putting them in an old pillowcase so we had something to eat when we get where we going. We said, "We're going to be moving. Mama's frying up a lot of chicken. Daddy must have gotten fired." That was how we knew we were going to another area. They didn't have unions in the coal mine at that time. I heard my father say, "Well, you don't know whether you'll be back or fired." My daddy would come home and say, "Well, we got fired today. The boss said he didn't want us." Then they had to go to another place and look for work until they finally got unions. I was a teenager. That was in Faraday, West Virginia—when he was working at the Pocahontas Fuel Company he joined the United Mine Workers.

Amonate and Faraday—Amonate was in Virginia, three miles—and when you get to the line, you could have one foot in Amonate and one foot in Faraday, West Virginia. All of that was where the miners that lived in Amonate had to come to Faraday—they would ride a bus to pick you up and take you to the mine.

Ten to twelve miles from us in War, West Virginia, the stores and restaurants were segregated, but our Pocahontas Fuel Company store was integrated. The company store, it had to be integrated, because everybody's time went in the same office. Upstairs were clothing and groceries and sundries, including a complete meat market. But down underneath of it was the restaurant where we would go and buy sandwiches or soup or whatever you want. And when we moved here [to Christiansburg], we hadn't been used to that, where you couldn't go. But it was still [better than] in Grundy, Virginia, about forty miles from there, where the colored couldn't go. They'd shoot at you just like you were a rabbit.

Opposite, top: Amonate tipple. *Eastern Regional Coal Archives, Bluefield West Virginia.*

Opposite, bottom: Faraday street scene, circa 1920s. *Eastern Regional Coal Archives, Bluefield West Virginia.*

Above: Faraday Store, Pocahontas Fuel Company, circa 1920s. *Eastern Regional Coal Archives, Bluefield West Virginia.*

Pocahontas Fuel Company had thirteen mines. A gentleman from Germany, Mr. Roncaglione, was the superintendent of the coal mines.[17] It was a rich company. It was just a few miles from Bramwell, West Virginia, where the millionaires lived.[18] But Pocahontas was where my husband was born—Pocahontas, Virginia—and that was where the head office of Pocahontas Fuel Company was.

Once every three months, tailors came to the company store. I came up like that in the coal field. We could have been like a lot of people. They didn't want it. When they would draw their money, they would go to the nearest town like War, West Virginia, or in Bluefield to the cheapest stores and buy the cheapest clothes, but we didn't. My mother always said, "You can always elevate yourself and make it better. It's up to you. You can go down or up. You're the person that has to decide that." Just because we were in a coal field, that didn't mean we didn't know how to dress.

MY MOTHER WAS A ROSA PARKS

*"My mother wasn't a show and tell person.
She was for real, and she did for people."*

Oh, what I was going to tell you was that all the time, from my grade school to high school, I went to the same school. We went from English [West Virginia] to grade school. When we moved from Excelsior [West Virginia], I was transferred back to Excelsior to grade school into high school. I went to the same school basically. We rode pretty close to fifteen miles every day. The thing that I had in mind to tell you: the bus would pick the colored children up first, which was around seven o'clock, and take us to school. Then when school let out, it would bring the White schoolchildren home first and then us last. I know you've heard it, but they say, "Last hired and first fired." Well, we were first to go to school and last to come back from school. That's just the way we were treated, and that happened all the way up through high school. That's the way it was.

It was when my mother's smaller children were in grade school and had to ride the same bus. They would have to go and wait until the teacher came in at eight o'clock. That's about two hours, waiting in the cold. She was tired. I never dreamed of that until these last years. I said, "Well, my mother was a Rosa Parks." She said, "I'm tired," and she pawned her sewing machine to Mr. Jesse Pew. I'll never forget him. He had a car with a rumble seat in the back. He picked the sewing machine up with another man helping him and put it in his car and let my mother have five dollars to pay somebody to carry her to the school board in Iaeger, West Virginia, to make her complaint. She went by herself. I didn't think too much of it, really, until Miss June [Sayers] wrote the letter to the Library of Virginia in Richmond for the "Strong Men and Women Award." I said, "That's how we can feel what happened to the colored race." We have strong colored—now we are saying Afro-American—women. But if you didn't have a strong mother, I can understand why you are like you are. We were just fortunate. And from what I have heard, the time frame was about a month. Somebody said, "Mama, there goes a McDowell County truck with lumber on it." That's when they started hauling the lumber to get ready to build a [Black] school, right there in Faraday, West Virginia.

Segregation/Jim Crow

"I have gone through a lot of things. I never try to hold it against people.
I just ask God to let me keep learning, and being patient with people."

We just knew our place. We couldn't go in hotels and sleep. We couldn't go in to eat in the restaurant that would serve you. You knew you couldn't sit down. You could go in and buy and come out. But some wouldn't even sell to you. That's where my cousin, my mother's cousin, and who looked White, would go and buy food for Daddy and them when they were trying to secure a job.

Education

Oh, well, let's put it this way: we knew not as much until we got in high school. We just knew we weren't to go there. Why? We didn't ask questions. But when you get in high school, that's when we really knew that we were going to a different school—we can't go to that school. Then you find out that some things [they had] in their school, the White school, you didn't have it in your school. We knew it was different, but people didn't make too much disturbance over it. It was leading up to where we did do it. But when I first started into grade school, it was just something—this is the way it is—and you accept it. In high school, we learned what it meant.

The reason I worked during my senior year in high school—my parents really didn't want me to do it—but they were not able to buy my class ring, and the class ring only cost $9.50. The mine was on a strike. It was during the [Great] Depression, 1939. I ironed for the outside superintendent, Mr. Barlow. The outside superintendent took care of the housing for the people that lived in this mining community. I was working for him and his wife. She would always have a bushel basket of clothes sprinkled. That's when people sprinkled clothes. And there were sheets, and it wasn't the kind of material we have today. I only got $1 a day, worked all day long for $1 in 1939. I approached them when I found out she needed someone to iron for her.

But I really didn't have to go the whole school term because our church missionary society found out that I was working. And when my mother and I went to a missionary meeting, after so many weeks that I had been working, the ladies in the missionary society put their money together and gave whatever I needed to get my ring and some other things I needed. I wrote it down here: "From that day, ever since that time, I feel happy about my life and my mother and father, the training that they gave us and taught us how to share with your friends and your family."

My mother did not start, as we call it, "missionary work" when she got married. She was doing that before she married my father. At that time, we did not have a tuberculosis home or hospital to go to, and people stayed in their home with tuberculosis. They would put them on the back porch and screen it in, and that person just stayed there until they died. You waited on them. So I learned through talking with her that she had worked with people as a teenager, helped bathe them and do things for them, given them their food, whatever they could eat, before she married my father. But after she was married to my father, she belonged to a missionary society in our church. And we believe in: if you or your family had an illness, you go there, and you help wash clothes, cook for them or do whatever you can.

My mother was just an outgoing, doing person for people. You see, some people do it just for show and tell. Like you used to do with your children when they go to school on Monday morning, had to have something for show and tell. My mother wasn't a show and tell person. She was for real, and she did for people. And it grew on just about all her children—we were the same. We believe in helping and doing things.

The missionary society was the church group. My parents were Baptists. But where I grew up, when you had a missionary society meeting, you may have any other church members and people come to your meeting. It was just a together community. And that's how I have always based my giving as well. As much as I have done during my lifetime came from the missionary society giving my mother the money and being taught how to share in the home. My parents tried to teach us, "If you can't share with your sisters and brothers in your own home, how can you share with other people?" So, as I told you before, my role model was my mother.

My mother was also a midwife. One of the older doctors, whenever he'd get a call he'd call my mother. We did not have telephones in the home. We had to go to the company store or either to the area where they had a chipper that washed the coal before the train came up to pick all the coal up to carry it to whatever state they were going to carry it to. I think it was two or three rings that was meant for the company doctor, and you mentioned the house number, and they would come. Doctors were doing house calls then.

And when someone was about to have a baby, the doctor would call and Mama would go and help him. He would come and ask her if she was busy.

VIRGINIA DEFENSE COUNCIL
IN COOPERATION WITH
VIRGINIA STATE DEPARTMENT OF HEALTH

Home Nursing Certificate

THIS CERTIFICATE IS ISSUED TO

Nannie May Hariston OF _Amonate, Virginia_

Tazewell COUNTY WHO HAS SATISFACTORILY COMPLETED THE VIRGINIA STATE DEPARTMENT OF HEALTH COURSE IN HOME NURSING TAUGHT IN CONNECTION WITH THE NATIONAL CIVILIAN DEFENSE PROGRAM. ANY SERVICES RENDERED IN THE HOME CARE OF THE SICK MUST BE ON A VOLUNTEER BASIS.

Coordinator Virginia Defense Council

State Health Commissioner

Date _January 5, 1942_

Class Instructor

This is not a Certificate for Practical Nursing

Home nursing certificate, Virginia State Department of Health, January 5, 1942. *Hairston family.*

If she wasn't, he'd say, "I'm leaving, and I think maybe in the next hour or two, or maybe in the next two days, I'll be back. And if you can help, clean her up." And if it was a person who didn't have someone to clean them up, the doctor would mention to my mother and an aunt of mine named Irene Berger, and they would go and clean up the person. And when it's time for her to have the baby, they would go back and forth if they didn't have someone in the home to help them. So that was her basic life all of her life until she got where she couldn't go. I feel that it was something that was meant for my mother to be.

In fact, I wanted to be a nurse. But my parents weren't able to send me to school. I do have a little certificate. I'll show it to you before you stop doing [this], if you write down for me to show it to you. In the 1940s, Pocahontas Fuel Company gave out a notice—anyone that wants to come and be trained to do nursing to help people in the community, because so many of the nurses had to go to the army—and they trained us. That's how I got my training of trying to help take care of the sick and got this certificate through Pocahontas Fuel Company.

Sports

There was a tennis court and a baseball field before we started playing baseball, and they had a field put where the Blacks could play in Faraday. As you remember me telling you, the company store was in Amonate, the post office was in Amonate, but the mines were in Faraday, and Amonate is in Virginia. Anyway, Amonate was where they had a tennis court, and we would look at people. When I saw the two Williams girls [Venus and Serena] playing tennis, I said, "If we'd had an opportunity to play tennis when we were coming up, we probably would have been good and could have played." But we had no way of playing.

But coming back to me playing, we couldn't play on the tennis court—it was for Whites, and the baseball field was also for Whites, before we got the one for us. And, believe it or not, I wish we had a picture of it, we had a theater in the coal field where we came from, but we couldn't sit where the Whites [were]. They had a section made for us—whoever built that theater on the coal field where we lived.

The baseball team eventually moved to Amonate, three miles away. That's where our baseball field was. It was a beautiful baseball field and had a grandstand that seated one hundred people or more paid for by the company.

When I was at home, though, before I got married, we had a team. One coal camp would play baseball against the other one. I think we played about fifty-five counties—it may be more now—in the state of West Virginia. That was our recreation with the men. Then, down through the years, the women decided that they wanted a baseball team, so they started playing baseball. They organized and had a manager, and whenever we went anywhere, we represented Faraday. The team of the men and the women were the same as the men that worked for Pocahontas Fuel Company. That's how you identified what team was playing against the other team—what company they worked for. Our team was called the Faraday Yellow Jackets. I was the youngest on the team.

We had baseball uniforms that were made by someone in the county. Back in the years we couldn't go swimming, but you know Whites, when you see them swimming, some of them had these one-piece suits on with the elastic that goes down to the knee? So we had those suits made, and then three or four young people like myself could play sports with them. I used to be a shortstop, and I'm left-handed. If you recall, I told you that the gentleman that bought the mines, Pocahontas Fuel Company, was from Germany, Mr.

Roncaglione. And whenever he had the opportunity, he'd come see the men play and the women play.

Since I've gotten grown, I've said, "Oh, I was just like the Globetrotters," and we didn't know anything about the Globetrotters. But [Mr. Roncaglione] would always ask, "Who is that playing shortstop?" And see, when you're playing shortstop, you're right between third base and second base. I had to turn all the way around when I'd get a ground ball to throw it to the first base. Everybody thought that was something. I never thought too much about it, about what I was doing, until one day, since I've been living here, I said wait a minute, "I was almost acting like a Globetrotter."

A Beautiful Life

"I just had a beautiful life, is the only way I can picture it."

Like I said, I had a beautiful life of being poor. I guess that sounds stupid to some people, if they hear you saying you had a beautiful life and poor. But what I'm saying, we had parents that taught us not to just feel sad for yourself because you don't have. What you do have, enjoy, and realize that someday, if you keep going to school and doing for yourself—and learn that you can't have anything in this life without working for it if you really want it to be your own. And so if you learn how to work—and then when you get where you can't work and you need help, then you're supposed to know how to go and address yourself about the issue to whoever's concerned.

So I just feel that I had a beautiful life growing up without a father that could read or write. Our parents taught us: "One day, if you keep trying, you can have a home of your own, and you can do this, but you won't have it unless you work." So we were taught to work and try to save. That's another thing—you may not have as much as Rockefeller, but you can have something, if you can be taught that you have to learn to know how to save.

I don't regret anything that happened in my life that I may have wanted to happen. I don't. Since my husband died, I think over the things in my life, of my married life with him for seventy years, and I just think of all the things. I can't think of anything that I can feel maybe we should have [done differently]. I just had a beautiful life, is the only way I can picture it. What I'm saying, when things came that we felt like it wasn't the best for us, we learned to accept it. That's one of the most important things: Learning what to accept and what not to accept.

Ever since I've been in the world, where I came from. I don't know about other states. I'm just talking about the part I grew up in—from Crumpler, English, Excelsior and Faraday and moved to Amonate when I got married. Three miles. That's the farthest I ever lived from my parents. I never had the opportunity to say, "I'm going home this summer." Then when we moved to Christiansburg, John brought them here with us.

Chapter 2

MARRIAGE AND MOTHERHOOD, 1941–1953

"Our life was filled with the joy of knowing that we had helped someone."

A GOOD LIFE

Nannie Berger married John T. Hairston on his twenty-first birthday, June 14, 1941, in Bristol, Tennessee. She was two months away from her twentieth birthday. They went to New York City for their honeymoon. Upon their return home, Nannie moved with John to Amonate, Virginia, next door to her in-laws. They had their first child, Catherine, in June 1942, and their second, Edwina, in October 1944. Both children were born at home and were difficult births.

Nannie settled into her life as a new wife and mother, and John worked for Pocahontas Fuel Company as a checkweighman and was the financial secretary for the Local Union No. 6633 of the United Mine Workers of America. One of the projects John was working on with a local UMW committee was to integrate the nearby Clinch River Medical Center. African American patients were treated at the clinic, but they were only allowed to stay overnight in the basement.

In addition to caring for her young family, Nannie volunteered with different community organizations, including the Order of the Eastern Star. Organizational meetings were held on different days of the week, and sometimes she hosted luncheons at her home. Learning from her mother, she was community-minded and helped those in need. She was also able to

Left: Nannie Berger, circa 1940. *Right*: John Hairston, Amonate, Virginia. *Hairston family.*

come close to her goal of becoming a nurse by completing a course offered by the Virginia State Department of Health for home nursing that was part of the National Civilian Defense Program (January 5, 1942).

John served in World War II and the Korean War. He was inducted into the segregated army on February 22, 1945. He went to basic training in Fort Jackson, South Carolina, and Fort McClellan, Alabama, and eventually was sent to Fort Lewis, Washington, where he was trained in demolitions and construction. He was still training when World War II came to an end in May 1945. He was assigned to the 41st Combat Engineer Battalion and sent to Germany for cleanup operations. In 1946, he was discharged from active duty, but he decided to stay in the army reserves.

He was home for a few years and went back to his work in the coal mine but was called up again when the Korean War broke out in 1950. By this time, the U.S. Army had been integrated by President Harry Truman's Executive Order No. 9981 (July 26, 1948): "There shall be equality of treatment and opportunity for all persons in the armed forces without regard to race, color, religion, or national origin." John served in the 25th Infantry Division in Korea, where he saw active combat. He was wounded in April

1951, hospitalized, shipped home and released from active duty in 1952 at the rank of staff sergeant. He received the Silver Star, the Purple Heart, and the Combat Infantryman's Badge because of his service against the enemy in a combat zone.

During the time that her husband served overseas, Nannie stayed in their home in Amonate with her in-laws next door and also spent time with her parents in Faraday. John had suggested that she may want to go to college at Bluefield State College, a historically Black college in nearby in Bluefield, West Virginia, like her sister Blanche. But she decided that she would rather stay home and raise her two children. She did exactly that, as well as volunteering with community organizations, her church and the schools. She got her driver's license. And in one case that was a precursor to her later civil rights activities, she had the bravery, skill and connections to help some laborers on a farm in Tazewell County get medical help and venture out into the community. Nannie Berger Hairston never lacked for energy and determination to right wrongs when she saw them.

When John returned from service, he went back to his work in the coal mines, but within a few months, the mines closed. John, fresh from his military experience in Europe, and Nannie, having handled matters at home during two wars, set out on a new path, in a new place, after just ten years of marriage.

John T. Hairston

"[John said] I feel sorry for the man who marries her."

Family Background

I met John T. Hairston in senior high school. The town where he lived was called Amonate, where I told you, the Pocahontas Company Store and the post office were. His father was a Methodist minister, and Tazewell is just like Montgomery County here. But Tazewell County did not have a school for Black children to go to, even by themselves, and you know they weren't permitted to go with White. We didn't have a school in Tazewell County.

So his parents and a lot of other parents, in order for their children to continue to go to school after they were in the seventh grade, going into high school, they had to go to West Virginia or no school. Their parents had to pay five dollars a month for each child that attended school. [John was the eldest of ten children.] And then they had to walk. It was over three or four miles. Anyway, whatever the mileage, they would have to walk from their home to the West Virginia line to catch the bus. Two or three other families did the same.

That's why it's so important, I feel, today, how people don't force their children to go to school, they have all the opportunity, and they just let them do what they want to do. I still go back to what Mrs. Clinton used to say: "It takes a village to raise a child," and it does. You can almost tell by the community, what comes out of it, what type of people that you have in your community. If it's one-sided, you're just taking care of your family and forget about the rest, and when I say your family, the poor people, whether White or Black, they're on their own, and you don't give them that much encouragement. So then your county grows up to be like a county in some other area of your state. It's because they aren't getting the training. We grew up in a community.

My husband's father, Samuel Wesley Hairston, died when John was five years old. In later years, his mother married Reverend John Patterson "Pat" Purcell [pointing to the photograph in *Colored* magazine, May 1946]. This is the only father that my husband ever knew, and this gentleman, Charlie Davis, was his dear friend. You see the tuxes they have on? The Pocahontas Fuel Company bought those for them. And when my father-in-law used to travel, they traveled in the Pullman. He was a Methodist minister and Mr. Davis was a minister, and they were close friends to the family. But he worked for the company longer than John's daddy. They both have tuxes on, the company paid for them, and they got this in this magazine.

They worked for the company store, and they saw that they got tuxedos and clothes to wear. You see what I'm saying? And my husband's mother taught them to work. I told you that he washed cars to get his money. His daddy could have bought it. But they did have a means of taking care of themselves because his mother had a boardinghouse. She had one house next to the house they lived in, which was an eight-room house, and kept boarders.

His parents had means. It was different from mine because they had jobs. His daddy had a job working for the company and then [was] a minister on top of that. He always had a job. He fired the furnace at the company store.

John Hairston and Janie Moore Hairston Purcell, circa 1939. *Hairston family*.

I don't know what his salary was. I just knew if you would walk in the store, he would be dressed. He had clothes he wore to work, but he had a tie on, and work shirts, but he had a tie. He was a very dignified person.

Courtship/Wedding

I don't know whether I ever told you the complete story. I mentioned it. I think I told you the other day about John with the football players, and he made a statement. I always think about his statement, and I tell people, I say, "You remember President Roosevelt, FDR said, 'All I have to fear is fear itself.'" I said, "But John T. Hairston said, 'I feel sorry for the man who marries her,'" because I was the type, like that stool there, instead of walking around it, I could just stand flat-footed and jump over it. I was kind of tomboyish. He had no idea.

We never dated in school. We were classmates. John was captain of the football team, and he invited me to the football banquet one year. Something happened between him and his girlfriend at the time, and John invited me. I was told by some of my classmates they would not go. But I thought it was nice, and some of my girlfriends were angry with me, and they were real close friends. They said, "If he is a classmate, I wouldn't go to this feast with him." But I did, after I asked my mother could I go.

The teachers, you know how they do in school, have a football team dinner. And as I said, John was the captain of the football team. This is the remark I made to some of the students, my classmates. I said, "Well, you know, we don't eat turkey but once a year," and you didn't. You had turkey for Christmas. If you had it for Christmas, you didn't have it for Easter, if you had it for Easter, you didn't have it for Christmas, vice versa. And then we had ham. Back then, people were raising their own meat, had these big country hams, and all that. I told them, I said, "Well, I'll get turkey more than one time this year, because the teachers are going to have all these big turkeys with the turkey dressing," which people don't make now. We buy dressing now, but back then, you know how people made their dressing, cornbread dressing. I said, "I'm going to enjoy myself."

But at the time, I didn't have a dress that you would like to wear to a banquet. We had a lady named Miss Sadie Jones. I'll never forget her. She had all kinds of clothes. Mama said, "Well, maybe Miss Sadie, if she has something, she'll let you wear it." And she did. I can't even remember what kind of dress it was, but it was appropriate. She let me wear the dress that I wore to the banquet for the football team, and John had nothing else to do with me after that was over. I wasn't dating him anyway, and there was never anything between us.

He never said anything to me after that until 1939. That [banquet] had to have been a year or two years before we graduated. And after that, in 1939—it was the first World's Fair in California, and he helped one of the schoolteachers, our music teacher and director of the Glee Club, Dr. Prince Ahmed Williams, drive to the World's Fair. When he came back, for some reason, he came to visit. A car stopped in front of our house, and it was John getting out. He said, "I just thought I'd come over and tell you about the World's Fair," and he did.

And after that, he came back the next week and the next week. I think the second or the third time, my mother said, "Is he still talking about the World's Fair?" I thought that was cute. John and I started dating for over a year and a half. And then, within two years, he proposed. He asked me about marrying him. I shooed him off and shooed him off. And we finally came to some kind of agreement.

But in the meantime, John was twenty years old. His mother said, at that time, I don't know if you can recall, it doesn't matter what age you are, but back in those days, you had to be twenty-one years old to go into the army. And she said, "You know you're not a man. If you were a man, they'd have had you in the army." Because when you get to be twenty-one, that's when they could draft you to go to the service. So she said, "I don't think you ought to get married until you get twenty-one years old, a man, and then you don't have that kind of money saved up." I'm listening to her talking.

And then he decided. I admired him. I didn't use that word, *admire*, but I said I think it's nice he listened to his mother. But everybody that knew us said, "You all will never wait on each other." And so we had a year. My mother couldn't afford a wedding. They didn't have the kind of money for a wedding. I got a dress, and my dress came from Sears Roebuck & Co. catalogue.

So, one day he and I were sitting, just like you and I here talking, and the next week he said, "You know, I'll be twenty-one years old next week." But as I said I had already bought my dress, had gotten a dress to be married in. It was blue. But in the meantime, it was funny. John came over and asked my mother and father, said, "Nannie and I decided tomorrow we're going to go and get married." They didn't object. We went to Bristol, Tennessee.

Honeymoon

We went to New York. One of his brothers let him use his car, and that's where we went. It was my first time being out of the state of West Virginia. We went to Radio City [Music Hall], and that's the first time I saw the Rockettes. And when you see the stage where they go, where they push a button somewhere and here the Rockettes come, that's what I tell anybody, that's who I saw first on my honeymoon trip. We went to the movies and a ballgame. I'm trying to think of the team that played. John had a sister and brother that lived out on Long Island, and we stayed with them. But no, we went to New York. And we knew where we were going, all the highlights. I can see them now, seeing those women coming out, the Rockettes. They could really dance. It was my first trip away from home and the first thing I saw in New York.

Coal Miner's Wife

"My husband would tell all the doctors at the hospital, he said,
'We all went in different colors but we all came out Black,' and that was true."

When we first got married, we got a house with three rooms. It was a kitchen, bedroom, and a living room, front porch and a back porch. As I mentioned, it was in Amonate. A bit later, John and I moved down next door to my mother-in-law and father-in-law because we could get a house with more rooms. My mother-in-law had water in her house. It came from a White family. I don't know if he was foreman or what he was in the mine, but he had water. It came right by my house and another Black woman's home to my father-in-law. And you remember my telling you my father-in-law fired the furnace in the company store, but he was a Methodist minister.

We didn't go to the hospital then. My first two children were born at home. Dy-Anne was born at Radford, and Colette was born over at Radford. But Catherine and Edwina were born at home. You'd call the doctor. When they felt like you were in labor and they think it wasn't time, they'd come back when you called them again. [My mother] was with me, and my mother-in-law was with me. I was in labor for two or three days. Well, that was the way it was. All people, Black and White, had the same [White] company doctor. That's all we ever had in the coal field. Dr. Massey was older, and Dr. Jackson was younger. They were the family doctors.

Amonate, circa 1920s. *Eastern Regional Coal Archives, Bluefield West Virginia.*

My days were just like I am here. Some days you go shopping wherever your closest town was, and the closest town to where we lived was Richlands, Virginia, which was at least ten miles, and War, West Virginia, was just about a mile from where I went to school, Excelsior High School. You belonged to different organizations, and you had certain days in the week you went. I was a great missionary worker. I got that from my mother. I learned how to do things in the community. But other than that, we had different organizations that people belonged to, and you'd visit. Some of them were with the church, like I was at Eastern Star, I belonged to them. And just like my life here, we had certain days that you had meetings. You knew when that was, and you invited people into your home for a luncheon. I had a typical lifestyle. It was not boring. And during those days, where I came from in West Virginia, the women didn't work like women work today. You stayed at home, you cooked, you cleaned your home and you had different things that you had to do in your home to keep your home going, as a normal wife would. Then if you didn't belong to anything, I don't know what life was like. I always have been in organizations all my life and doing volunteer work. So I had a busy life, and I don't call it an unhappy busy life. I had a life because I loved people more than just myself and my family.

Where I was reared [in Faraday, West Virginia]—at the Pocahontas Fuel Company Store—was integrated. We had some of the best food, clothes and doctors. We had no complaints. That's what I was saying—in the coal mines where I came from, we all had the same doctor's office. It wasn't you're Black and you're White. It didn't go that way. My children didn't know anything about [segregation] until we went somewhere out of town. For example, when the United Mine Workers were having a convention, we had to go find a Black motel or a tourist home they called it, and we had to find where Blacks stayed. You couldn't go where the Whites stayed, and we learned this is not a place for us to go. And when we got on a bus, if we were riding the bus, we knew the last four seats in the back of the bus [were for us], and if the bus up here was filled up and you got on the bus, and unless you were a very nice White woman, you came back there for us and I would have to stand up and give you my seat.

But we had a good life. [Even after our children were born], we went to church, and we went to football games like I always liked. Now I can't go, and I have to look at them on TV. My school was in Excelsior, and when they had football games we went, and then Bluefield State College, was in Bluefield, West Virginia, when they had homecoming games we went. Our life never stopped. My parents or his parents would take care of the baby if we wanted to go to a football game.

[I remember one time while we were living] in Amonate, though, John and I were going to a ballgame. He kept blowing the horn, wanting them to come give us gas, and they were just standing [there]. He was blowing his horn again, and he maybe blew the horn two or three times. I said, "Sugar, the next thing you're going to see is a high-powered rifle pointing at you. We better leave, because they aren't coming." They never did come out. It was our first and only time we ever went anywhere and they wouldn't serve us gas. At that time, they used to pump you the gas, and they just stood and looked at us and never did come over to sell us gas. We have been down through Alabama and Georgia and places in Mississippi, North Carolina, where things happened. But that happened between Amonate, Virginia, and Richlands, Virginia. We were on our way to Kentucky to a ballgame.

Union Man

My husband was a United Mine Worker. He worked inside the mines, I'd say, approximately ten years. I have pictures of him being the checkweighman job in the coal field. The coal company, at that time—it's different now. The coal company would have a company man when the car of coal comes out. Then he's on one side of the car, and on the other side of the car is the union man. That lets you know it checks out, if it's three tons or whatever. Their word was against each other.

Once my husband disagreed with the amount of coal that the company checkweighman said it was. They were held up long enough for the checkweighman to call the company. They called my father-in-law because John was holding up production. John told his father, "I'm being paid to protect the miners. And he was putting down the wrong weight. I know I am right." It ended up that John was right. Now that process of weighing the coal is automated. You've got to be a strong person to represent people in certain areas. John was the union man. That was his job up until he went to World War II. And then when he came back, he stayed in the reserves and went to the Korean War. Then he was wounded.

He was on the United Mine Worker committee that was working, trying to get—well, you know what we were called back then, colored people—the Richlands, Virginia Clinic [Clinch River Medical Center] to allow us on all the floors. We had to stay in the basement of the hospital if you got sick. You couldn't stay up where the Whites were. I don't care how poor or rich they were—if they were White, they were there in the hospital, and we had to stay in the basement.

The War Years

"Sugar, why do you stay in the reserves?
You love the army better than you do me?"

When John was called to go to World War II, he went to Mr. Roncaglione and spoke to him and told him that he was going to be going in service, and said, "I would like for my wife to stay in the house or to have her own home with the two children until I get back. And I would like for you to put water in the house." And they did. He said, "Some planks on my sidewalk are coming loose, and you all need to come and fix those." And it was. You know how planks that get where if you step on it in the middle, it won't fly up, but if you get too close to this edge and this edge it would come up with the nails still holding, but not enough. So they came and put a new walk in.

I'm just showing you how things work, and it was not going through a lot of argument. It was done. Mr. Roncaglione told my husband, "As long as she lives a decent life, not upsetting the community with different people going in the home and doing things, she'll have a home until you get back."

That's where I lived until my husband came back from Germany. But I also went back home. My husband told my father, he said, "I'm bringing her back home to you until I get back from the service." I was treated just like I was never married. I had two children, Catherine and Edwina. My father would say, "Now, you've got these two children you know you have to take care of them. You've got a home here. You don't have to worry about anything." I had my house, but I stayed just as much with Mama and them than I did at my own house. It was a blessing.

Then John was home a year or two and was called back because he stayed in the reserves. I said, "Sugar, why did you stay in the reserves? You love the army better than

John Hairston, Korean War. *Hairston family.*

you do me?" He said, "Well, how are we going to protect you? I guess I love the army in a way, because I'm trying to protect you and the other people [in the country]." And that was the end of it. It wasn't long before he was getting a greeting from Uncle Sam. He got wounded in Korea. He has a Purple Heart and got one of the highest medals, a Silver Star. He never talked about his time in the service either during World War II or the Korean War.

I found out what a platoon is. His platoon, thirty-some men, they all were colored. There were two hundred and some men in his company. But at the end, it was only three left. I'll show you the picture of the other two men before you stop coming here. One was in Clemson, South Carolina, and the other one lived in Philadelphia. Then there were three men that were left in that company. [It was an] all-Black, all-colored company.

John did tell me one story. When he was coming home from wherever he was coming from, on a furlough, and the White conductor told him—he was trying to get to the part—you know, Black people had to always get to the car next to the engine. He told him, said, "Come on in here, young man, and sit down." That's exactly what this conductor told my husband. John said only White people were there, and he just figured it would cause confusion. So he was going on through, trying to ask him whatever he had asked the conductor. I guess how far he had to go to get to the car, where he could sit. [The conductor] told him, "Just sit here." That was a story he told, and he never mentioned anything else about it, but that was one thing that happened to him coming home on that trip.

There's one thing that happened to me when John was injured. My home economics teacher, when I was in school, asked me if I would help chaperone some children to the West Virginia state capitol, which is in Charleston, West Virginia. They were taking some Excelsior schoolchildren, which was about maybe one hundred and some miles from where we lived, on a tour. They were taking a busload. So okay, this is the front of the bus. This is the bus driver. Two teachers sitting there, and this is where you come up the aisle of the bus. And I'm sitting right here. It's one seat, as you know, like when you're going to step out to go out the bus, and I was sitting there. The very day that my husband got wounded, I don't know how I did it, but I caught myself, I jumped, and whichever way I hollered, I don't know what sound I made. And Mrs. Carroll said, "What's wrong?" I said, "John went over me in a airplane." I guess I had dozed off to sleep, sitting up on the bus and then when this happened I jumped.

Well, we were gone two days. When we got back home, my husband— that's what I try to tell people. It depends on who you are, what you learn, who you know and how you do something. He had a friend. It had to have been somebody in the office, and knowing my husband, I guess he made friends if he got a chance to make friends with someone. And he told him to cablegram the store, Pocahontas Fuel Company, and to tell them to tell his father that he'd been wounded, but not bad as he may think, and he's okay. He wasn't okay, but he was letting us know that he had been injured.

I found it out from the army—it was either three months or four months later. I can't recall. I had gone somewhere, to Huntington, West Virginia, to visit my sister, and when I came back, Bobbie Lee, one of my sister-in-laws, said, "Some army men came over here in a big black Packard car looking to tell you from Tazewell—that's the county seat—that your husband had been wounded." I had already known.

Helping a Family of Farmworkers in Tazewell

"It doesn't seem real."

I decided one day that I would go to Tazewell, Virginia, to a farm, to find out for myself if [there] actually were people working there who were treated like slaves. I had heard that down through the years. So one day, I decided that I would go. My husband, John, was in Korea. I did not ask anyone to go with me, but I asked my father-in-law's chauffeur who carried him back and forth to work at Pocahontas Fuel Company's store in Amonate, if he would take me to Tazewell. He did not ask me why I was going, and I did not mention it to him. I told him, when we got into Tazewell, I would like to go by this farm. As I entered into the first gate, the guard asked me why I was there. I mentioned that I had heard there were "slaves" there.

By that time, a young woman appeared with a badly bloodshot eye. During those years, we didn't have milk in cartons like we have now in the plastic. It was a milk jar, and a jar broke. When the glass broke, it jumped up and it hit her eye. The rest of the workers were very dirty, their hair needed to be combed and groomed—and that did not happen. I'm sure they looked that way, as far as I know, from the time I met them, every day was the same lifestyle for them. Their hands were scaly-like, no lotion was used on them. And my feeling was that if the people that they were carrying that milk to knew how the people looked that were working on the farm and how they were being treated, I'm just wondering would there have been enough people to go to the source to have it changed. It's almost an unbelievable story.

So I told the guard. I didn't ask. I said, "I will be back to see if you all have carried her to a doctor." I went back the next day. They didn't say one word to me about leaving or going or anything. Only thing that I know is after that they gave my father-in-law the word that the workers could come to church. I told you my father-in-law was the preacher at the Methodist church.

And just like you see cattle going to the stock market here in Montgomery County, they rode—oh, I can see them now—standing up in the cattle truck. And when they got into church, they smelled. Can you imagine what a barn smells like? I mean, you work around that and don't bathe every day, or no days? That was the experience. And then they started letting them come to church. And then when one got sick, they would call [her father-in-law], and he would tell them about the doctors or whatever. That doesn't seem real, does it? But that was the story, honey, just as true as I'm sitting here looking at you.

What an experience. What made me do it has always just been a puzzle in my later years of life. I didn't think anything of it. It was something I heard about, and I wanted to see for myself, and I just took up enough courage to ask Mr. King to take me over because I didn't have a car. I didn't ask my father-in-law, and he didn't ask me. Because I felt like if I did, he would say,

"Wait, darling, you need to have somebody to go with you." After that, I just saw [the farmworkers] whenever they came to church. And after they started going to church, they saw a different life.

THE MINES CLOSED

"We went to work, and they just said you're not working anymore."

A few months after John returned from overseas, the mines closed down. They didn't tell anybody that they were going to close. You may have heard me say they had crossties like this. I thought someone had gotten killed. If someone gets killed on the nightshift, the day shift doesn't go to work. Or if the dayshift gets killed, the night shift doesn't go in. He said no. The crossties were like this. They just closed it down. And when I hear people talking about different companies, I say, "We experienced that." You know, sometimes you hear them say, "We went to work, and they just said you're not working anymore." That isn't a new thing. It happened to us in 1953.

Chapter 3

JIM CROW, 1953–1964

Christiansburg, Virginia

"Always remember this: Where you could go, I couldn't."

THE NAME OF THE GAME

The Pocahontas Fuel Company mine in Faraday, West Virginia, closed in 1953. Soon afterward, John and Nannie moved their family to Christiansburg, Virginia. In enterprising and resilient fashion, after the abrupt closing of the mine, John immediately went to Christiansburg and got a job at the Radford Army Ammunition Plant, and he got a job for Nannie's father there as well. The plant was also called Hercules, after the Hercules Powder Company, which first bought it. John was also able to find a home on a hill outside of the town that was on just under ten acres with a barn and orchards, as well as room for a garden, surrounded by the Blue Ridge Mountains in the distance.

The Hairstons established a multigenerational household that, in addition to their two young daughters, included Nannie's parents, an aunt and her sister Rosa's two children while Rosa was enrolled at Bluefield State College. And just two short months after moving to Christiansburg, their third daughter was born. That made ten in the family. There were various other family members who lived with them at times. It was a close-knit extended family, and when her parents moved into their own home, it was right next door.

The house and property had a rich history even before the Hairstons bought it. The property was originally owned by Walter McNorton, who was enslaved as a child at the Smithfield Plantation in Blacksburg, Virginia. When James Patton Preston, former governor of Virginia and owner of Smithfield, died and his estate was divided, Walter was ten years old and was sent to Preston's daughter Jane Preston Gilmer. He then went to her home in Pittsylvania County, where he married Eliza Perry in 1859, and stayed until he was emancipated in 1865. The couple left Pittsylvania County after the Civil War and by 1867 had settled in Montgomery County. Walter worked as a carpenter in and around Montgomery County and gradually built up his landholdings. Between 1876 and 1886, he bought three contiguous pieces of land north of Christiansburg totaling about 12.5 acres.

After Walter died, Eliza sold the land to the couple's two children: Robert Cutler McNorton and Nancy R. "Nannie" McNorton Reynolds. Nannie Reynolds lived in Danville with her husband and sold her half of the land to Cutler. Robert Cutler McNorton married Lou Ella Stratton, who taught at the Christiansburg Institute for many years, and the couple had a son named Cutler Reynolds McNorton, who went by C. Reynolds McNorton (1901–1985). He inherited the property when Robert Cutler McNorton died in 1932, and he held on to it until his mother died in 1953 because she was still living there. It is unclear when the house was built, but according to Dy-Anne Hairston Hash, it was a Sears kit house. Those were built between 1908 and 1942. In September 1954, Reynolds McNorton sold most of the homeplace (8.3 acres) to John and Nannie Hairston.[19]

Christiansburg itself has an important place in African American history. It is the site of the Christiansburg Institute (CI). The school was founded in 1866 by Captain Charles S. Schaeffer, a former Union soldier and Baptist minister from Philadelphia. Schaeffer was working for the Freedmen's Bureau when he came to Christiansburg to educate the newly freed slaves. It was the first and only African American school and college in Southwest Virginia. Another major milestone for the institute came in the 1890s when Booker T. Washington, founder of the Tuskegee Institute, became an advisor there. In the 1950s, when the Hairstons arrived, CI still functioned as the school for African Americans in Christiansburg and surrounding areas.

Christiansburg, like many other southern towns in the Jim Crow era, had a segregated area downtown with thriving Black-owned businesses. One was the Eureka Hotel on Depot Street, which was featured in *The Negro Motorist Green Book* and owned by Rae and Burrell Morgan. The Morgans

Students at Hill School, High Street, Christiansburg, 1930–31. *D.D. Lester Collection, Montgomery Museum.*

S.B. Morgan and Burrell Morgan, *Roanoke Times*, 1988. Permission received to use photos. *Virginia Deal Lawrence Collection, Roy Kanode.*

also owned a gas station, grocery store, barbershop, beauty parlor, café and taxi service, owned also with Burrell's brother S.B. Morgan. The area was a vibrant community nexus for decades, from the 1930s to at least the 1970s.[20]

Even with the CI and thriving Black business district, Christiansburg was a southern town, and the discriminatory policy of Jim Crow was the written and unwritten law of the land. The Hairstons' lives in Faraday and Amonate, West Virginia, had also been circumscribed by racism, of course, but the Pocahontas Fuel Company was in some ways integrated and thus they were somewhat shielded from the worst of Jim Crow. Moving to Christiansburg, Virginia, in the middle-1950s, though, put them squarely in the middle of it.

Nannie encountered the harsh conditions almost immediately upon arriving in their new community. After giving birth to her first two daughters in Amonate at home, she gave birth to Dy-Anne at the Radford Community Hospital approximately twenty miles away, the closest hospital that would accept African American patients overnight. She recounts the experience in the African American ward as degrading and unclean; she was worried for the health of her newborn. When Colette, her fourth and final child, was born in 1960, she spoke to her doctor, Dr. Glenn Claire Hall Jr., and made sure that she would be in a private room.

It wasn't only the medical system that was segregated. Until the Civil Rights Act of 1964 was passed, schools, restaurants, businesses, colleges and universities—in fact, most public places—were segregated. And it took many years after 1964 that the area became truly integrated. Nannie recounts stories about being refused service at local restaurants, cafés and pharmacies and the impact that had on her young children.

In addition, there were not a lot of options for employment for African American women. Nannie had never worked outside the home until she moved to Christiansburg, but she now felt she wanted to contribute to the family finances. The first job she had was as a maid, making fifty cents an hour. That didn't last long. She went on to become an insurance agent for Virginia Mutual Benefit Life Insurance Company. She was the first Black woman hired at the Christiansburg Garment Company (also known as the Blouse Factory) and, indeed, brought in several of her friends to work there. There were some short-term and temporary positions she held at Virginia Tech, including a dormitory cook and library associate. She eventually went to work for the Radford Army Ammunition Plant in 1963 as a custodian.

During these years, John was also ambitious and was a good provider for his growing family. He left his job at Radford Army Ammunition Plant when he found a better opportunity as a transportation postal clerk with the U.S. Post Office. Part of his responsibility included traveling by train to transport the mail, and in 1960, there was a train wreck and he was badly injured. He recovered, but he wore a back and leg brace after that and turned his attention to service and the nonprofit world.

HOMEPLACE

"It was God who blessed us with it."

We moved to Christiansburg in July 1953. A Black man, Mr. Reynolds McNorton, owned the property. His mother had recently died, and they were going to sell and leave here. Rae Morgan, who owned a restaurant on Depot Street, along with her husband, Burrell Morgan, said, "He's going to sell, but I have no idea who he'll sell to. No colored person. It'll probably be a White."

That's the name of the game, sweetheart. She was right. Mr. McNorton was Black, but that didn't matter. That was the history of our life, and we knew that. But it doesn't stop some people from trying. You know, being Black is a different story from being a Caucasian, especially the poorer you are, the worse off. And then when you're in the upper grade, you're still on a level that you have to go through a lot to get where you are. Oh, this place looked like a wilderness, all the trees up in here, and an apple orchard in front of it.

But anyway, John asked Mr. McNorton to sell to him. He said, "I have to think about it. But right now, if Mr. I. Hylton wants it, this is the first person." Mr. Hylton owned the apple orchard, and they're White. "If he doesn't want it, I'll sell to you." I was like "Doubting Thomas" in the Bible. I said, "You believe that, John?" He said, "Well, you're just like these other people saying he's going to sell to Whites." I said, "I just have a feeling he's not going to sell to us." And then John had such a belief in it, I wouldn't even ask a question.

John told Mr. McNorton, "I don't want to lease it for two years. I want to lease it a year at a time because I have to be still looking for somewhere for my family in case you contact someone and they want to buy it, then I've got to find somewhere to go." When the year was almost up, he called John, saying, "I've been talking with my wife off and on." He didn't mention Mr. Hylton. I'm sure if he had asked him, he didn't want it. The conversation didn't come up. He said, "Can you meet me at the courthouse?" It either was at nine or ten o'clock, whatever it was, and said, "We are ready to sell."

Months after that, Mr. [Marshall] Tolliver, a deacon at Schaeffer, came here and said, "Brother John, guess what Brother S.B. Morgan said to me. He said, 'I can't understand Mac selling to those foreigners.'" I've been called everything, but never been called a foreigner until I got to Montgomery County. I thought that was something. And to be truthful, a lot of people felt that way. I can understand why they felt the way they did. Here's a gentleman who's been going to church with them all his life, I guess. And Mr. Helvey, one of our neighbors, told me one time, "I think I can tell you this now." On this side of the railroad there were no colored people living. He said, "My oldest son said, 'It's Indians that live over there now.'" He was referring to us! Nobody could figure how we got this place. We had just come here from West Virginia, but it was God that blessed us with it.

I have been here sixty-three years. John and I were fortunate to get this place. As I started telling you before, my husband told my parents, "I would like for you all to come and live with us. I have found a house, and that home could be made for all of us at this time, because it's going to be hard for us to have to come back to you, you have no children here, all your other children are in the city, and you have no one to drive you or take you somewhere, and so, we would like for you to come and live with us."

Hairston home, Christiansburg, Virginia, 2023. *Sheree Scarborough*.

In the meantime, he had never discussed that with me. He just came and told me one day, "Nan, the way I see it, your parents are going to have to have us to take care of them by going out and seeing if they need to go to the doctor, and I have asked them to come with us. Now, you're going to have to give up cooking." I said to myself that won't be hard. I was within two months of having Dy-Anne.

So we came here together, and it was my mother, my father, and an aunt, who hadn't walked in twenty-some years, and my mother's third daughter [Rosa]'s two children. Rosa was in Bluefield State College. That was five. John was six, and I was seven. My two girls made nine, and when Dy-Anne was born, that made ten. Then I had a sister to come to visit us, and her three girls wanted to spend the summer. Then when the summer was over, time to go to school, they asked their grandmother, which is my mother, could they stay here and go to school. And she replied, "No. You have to ask your Uncle John. I'm just staying here with them. They are letting us stay."

But coming back to this place, I feel that God saw the need where my parents had to have somewhere to live, we had to have somewhere to live, and within two days after they were cut off from working in the coal mine, in two days, my husband had a job, the second day after he was cut off in the mine. He came here to the Radford Arsenal (Radford Army Ammunition Plant) and got a job, and then he was told about this place.

So, coming out of a community where you could shake hands with your neighbors on each side if you put your hands out the window, to here where I felt like Mama and I would never get used to being here by ourselves. But it came to be one of the most beautiful lives that anyone would want to have, raising a family, meeting people and then being involved in a community. We were accepted as well in the Caucasian community. We had been told by some people that our neighbors "weren't going to treat you all like they treat the McNortons, because they've been there all their lives." We never had a problem.

It just shows you never know how God—where he places you when you ask him and tell him that you want to have a good life—what's in store for your life. Our life was already picked out for us, and we didn't realize that coming to Montgomery County. We were doing some things in West Virginia like we have done here, but not as great.

Town

"We just always knew our place."

My children didn't really know about segregation until we came here and went to Thompson-Hagan Drugstore. It was near where First National Bank is now—right next door to it as you go into town on the right side was Thompson-Hagan Drugstore. And when the Whites would be there eating their lunch, Catherine and Edwina would say, "Mother, can we go get a grilled cheese?" I said, "No, you aren't going out here on the street eating a grilled cheese, and I'm not going to have you standing up in this drugstore eating, and you cannot sit." "Why?" they asked. I used to tell people, "Sweetheart, I was told when I was taking geometry in school it teaches you to reason. And I said, "No, it didn't teach me to reason like my children taught me." "Mother, why? Why we can't eat? Why can't we go over there?" I said, "Because you're colored, and we're not allowed."

You knew your place. Always remember this: Where you could go, I couldn't. You felt welcome. You can come to my place. But when it came down to me going to your place, a different story. You can see, down

West Main Street, Christiansburg, March 25, 1956, showing original Thompson-Hagan Drug building beside Roses. *D.D. Lester Collection, Montgomery Museum.*

through the years, what was going on. This town wasn't really designed to have a lot of Black people, because [after] slavery time, we're still here. Look how long. I can talk about my family more than I can any. When my children Catherine and Edwina graduated from high school, and you try to get them a job, that wasn't somewhere working in a restaurant, it was difficult. Mrs. Cameron had a place and S.B. [Morgan], but we didn't have too many Black people. Most of the businesses were run by [White] families, so we didn't get jobs. You just had jobs cleaning houses, and that was it when I came here.

But it was a strong foundation with Mr. Reynolds, Reverend Calloway, Mrs. Calloway and Mr. Sam Clark [in our local NAACP]. I can name all those older people. They were strong people, and they had nice personalities. Everybody can't deal with hate as well as some, and we all know that. They didn't let people run over them, but they had a way of knowing how to deal with people to achieve what they wanted.

Childbirth

"My doctor told me: 'No, we're not going to take you home.
We're going to move her.'"

We couldn't stay in the hospital overnight here in Montgomery County. If you didn't have a hospital for Blacks, you didn't have it. But we could go to Radford to the hospital. When I went to the hospital with Dy-Anne [in 1953] at Radford [Community Hospital], when it's time to feed your baby, I wasn't in the area with the Whites. I was in this one great big room. They called it a ward. I don't care if you had syphilis, pneumonia, gonorrhea, whatever—everybody was in that ward. When the time came for you to feed your baby, here they came with your baby. That's what I faced with my third child. They had one ward for Black women and one ward for Black men. And that wasn't only here. That was in Bluefield, West Virginia, and Richlands, Virginia, too. In Richlands they put us in the basement. But that's the way it was. It was like that all over the country.

And just before I had Colette [in 1960], when I got ready to leave the doctor's office, after I had my examination, he said, "You may come back earlier than you think." My doctor asked me, "Do you have any questions?" I said, "I do." I said, "With my third child, when I came here, I had to go in a big room. This is where you carry our babies, the Black baby has to come, and I have to be in the ward with all the women with all the things. I don't want to be found in the room in the situation that I had with my third child."

Leggett's Department Store had just finished building a room for the hospital. And when Colette was born, they put me in this room they just finished—Leggett's—that's how I know the name of it, it is where I was put. No integration, no nothing, we just talked and that's what happened. The White woman that was in the next room over was hollering and crying, "I

Radford Community Hospital, circa late 1940s. *Radford Public Library.*

don't want that N-word beside me! I don't want that N-word!" That's what I heard, and I said, "Well, you just let me go home." He said, "No, we're not going to take you home. We're going to move her." So they had to move her to another part of the area because she was hollering. S.B. Morgan, who had the taxicab for Blacks had a daughter who had a baby at the same time and we were put in that new area. There was a day between the births of our children.

DAY WORK

"Nannie's a good worker and she knows how to do things,
but she's not like the rest of the colored women that come here."

Do you know what they were making when I came here, being a maid? If you got seventy-five cents an hour, you were lucky. I did that before I went to be an insurance agent. I said, "Mama, we don't have enough curtains. The curtains here don't fit the windows. We need some more curtains. Our curtains in West Virginia don't look good at these windows." She said, "We just have to wait, sweetheart, until we get enough money." I said, "Well, why don't you let me go, when the doctor releases me, and you're going to take care of the baby, I'll go and do some day work." I said, "You know, I've never done it." She said, "Well, you clean up your own house. That's all you're going to be doing anyway. I guess if you want to go and try, but see what your husband says first." And he said, "Well, if that's what you want to do, Nan, go ahead, but you don't have to. If you just be patient, we'll get to that. Everything will fall in place when it's time for it." But I drove our car to work over here where the bed-and-breakfast is now.[21] I worked for Mrs. [Mary Etta Boyd] Harless two or three months for fifty cents an hour.

This is the first thing that happened to me in her home. Her back porch extended out to the wall, and they had a board that went across like that corner there and a board there. When I came here, people didn't have an oil furnace. They all had coal furnaces, back in the '50s. They hadn't got to the oil and gas yet. But they had scuttles for coal, shovels to move snow, for whoever was helping them do that on the back porch, and that's where I had to eat. So on the first day I was there, she said, "Nannie, aren't you going to eat?" I said, "If I have to eat out there, no, ma'am, I'm not hungry. I don't care to eat out there." So I didn't eat. I guess it went two or three days. When

I got home I said, "Mama, when we get these curtains, I'm going to quit those people. They're something else."

Well, when I went back in, and you know how they have these tables with the elephant feet. She had a round dining room table with the elephant feet in the kitchen. This wasn't in her dining room. She had a square one in the dining room. Then in the kitchen, a big coal stove over here. She didn't have an electric stove. I was there about three days, before that week was gone, and she said, "Nannie, if you want to eat now, you don't have to go out." I said, "I'm really not too hungry now." But it seems like the next day or two, I ate a sandwich or something. I had sense enough to be halfway decent since she went that far. She figured out that I wasn't going to eat in that corner, and that's when that stopped.

She would always give me bags of old linens and things. My mother taught us whenever anyone gives you something—always take it. And when we were growing up, if people gave her clothes and we said, "Mama, we don't want to wear that," we had to wear it to church whether you wanted to or not to let Miss So-and-So see it. She taught us when people give you something try to show that you appreciate it. Because sometime maybe you end up, you get something better.

I said, "Well, I'm grown now." Whenever I would leave, Mrs. Harless would say, "Well, Nannie, I see you didn't take the package. I left some things for you." I said, "Mrs. Harless, I'm going to tell you, I was taught to take things when people give to me. But that first package you gave me, everything in it was half rotten." You know, the material, she had it so long. I'm talking about clothes or pillowcases. I said, "I don't need to take it home and put it in my trashcan. You can just put it in yours." Oh, sweetheart. So I'm saying that to let you know what she said about me.

She offered my services to her friends. One of her friends was having a party, and I knew how to make ham biscuits. And she said, "I think my girl, she knows how to do everything, just about." So when I went to

Bell given to Nannie Hairston from Mary Etta Boyd Harless. The bell was Mrs. Harless's grandmother's and was supposedly used during slavery. *Sheree Scarborough.*

her, and came back the next day, well, the person that I was working for, she was very nice. And then the next person that needed me. If you ever go to Roanoke Street you see those small white houses on the right, those used to be Roberts Motel. So I was working for Mrs. Robinson. She just died a few years ago. She said, "Now Nannie, you don't have anything to do for the next hour and a half or two hours," whichever way it was. I think I went to work at seven o'clock. "And then you can fix Mr. Robinson's lunch." I said, "Well, I can go home then. I have a new baby, and I can go home and see if my mother needs anything from the store or something that I can go and pick up for her and come back." "Oh," she said, "you see those steps over that little house out there that goes up?" It had a place, you go up about thirteen or fourteen steps, where they used to go and look out at everything. "You could go over there and stay." And she said, "Well, when Nathan and Verna worked for me, they would go there and stay." I said, "Do you pay me for sitting up there?" She said, "No." I said, "Well, I'm not staying." She said, "Well, you came here to work."

I said, "Mrs. Robinson, I want my pay for the hours I've been here. I'm not sitting down here waiting for two hours or an hour and a half, when I could run home and see if my mother wants something or just look at my baby or whatever." I said, "I'm not Verna." So she tells Mrs. Harless. And when I went to work the next day to Mrs. Harless's, my regular job, she was just talking and talking and finally she said, "Nannie—" whatever Mrs. Robinson's name was, she called her by her first name. "She said that you were not the average colored woman." I said, "What'd she mean by that?" "You talked back to her." I said, "I don't understand when you say talk back. I answered her." She said, "Well, I have already told Patty—" Miss Patty liked me—she was her daughter-in-law. Mrs. Harless liked me. Patty told me, she said Mrs. Harless said, "She's a good worker and she knows how to do things, but she's not like the rest of the colored women that come here."

I'm going to tell you why she said that. One day she was talking to me, and some people had had a fight on Depot Street, colored people, and they were in the church, they were church people and had a falling out. That can happen to anybody. And she asked me about it. I said, "I don't know anything about it. I live out of town on 460," Blacksburg Road, they called it. And she said, "I thought maybe you knew about it. I just asked you." I said, "Where is your telephone book, Mrs. Harless?" She said, "I don't know." So Patty, a very young woman, she came in the room and she said, "Patty, Nannie wants the telephone directory. Do you know where it is?" And she said yes. She got it, handed it to me. I said, "I don't need it." I said,

"Mrs. Harless, you know the lady's name. You can call her. She's in the telephone directory, and she'll tell you what you asked me."

From that day on, sweetheart, she never asked me any more questions. She said, "I can understand now where you're coming from." I said, "No, I never worked for any people. My parents told us if we went to visit—" and I taught my children that, that if I send my children in your home to play with your children, don't come back telling me what went on at home. "Whatever you saw let it stay there; and what's here let it stay here. You're going to play." I was taught that, so it's still in me. They knew everything that happened from one maid's house, wherever there was a maid, they go and tell. I said, "How do these people know all of the other folks' business?" Come to find out, they ask the maids, and that's how they kept the conversation at the card game. Well, I went over here to the [Christiansburg] garment factory and applied for a job.

Christiansburg Garment Company

"Do you want to help yourself for tomorrow or just for today?"

[I decided I would] go there to get a job. Mr. [William] Phillips was the manager. He said, "Well, we don't have an opening." I said, "Can you leave your name on a list?" And he said, "No, we don't do that." I said, "Oh, thank you." Then I went back the next week and carried two or three more women with me. And when I went back the next week, the second or third week, he hired us at the garment factory. I had never been in one. He hired us and we were with them in the same big room, but we were over here. It was four or five of us Afro-American women. We were in this little corner.

Well, after a month or two, it was time for the picnic. So I asked the question, "Where do you have your picnic?" And one of the girls was nice. You know, you're always going to meet somebody nice, I don't care what race you meet. She told us. So the next day, a week or so before the picnic time, Mr. Phillips came to me, "Since you're the one that's responsible for these young women coming here with you, and you're young, I want you to know that you cannot have your family to come to the picnic and you can't come, because they don't want you to come and have dinner or lunch at the picnic with them." I said, "Well, isn't that the policy that you have?" See, I knew where he was coming from, but I acted like I didn't.

He said, "But that's just the way it is. What I'm going to do, you tell me how many are in your family and get the numbers on a paper from the other ladies how many are in their family, and I'll give you a certain amount of money." It was way up there. It wasn't $50. It was something like $200 or $300 if you had five or six in your family. And we had a big sum of money that was coming to us. I said, "Well, as far as I'm concerned, Mr. Phillips, I don't want the money. I came here to work, and I don't have to go to the picnic." He said, "Well, this is the way it is."

So, I go back to Miss Jones and all the other women. I can't remember their names now. Most of them are dead. I said, "He's going to give us money for however many are in our family where we can go and have our own picnic." I told them whatever amount it was, and one of them said, "Oh, boy, we'll have a good time. That's a lot of money, isn't it?" I said, "Yes, but our purpose is not for that. We came here to get a job and to work and try to help take care of our family, and we didn't come here for this. If they would allow us to go to the picnic, it would be fine. But to have it like they have it? I don't want it. I don't want the money, and I could use it." And one of the ladies said, "Oh, we'll just take the man's money, and we don't care." I said, "Well, you think about it. Do you want to help yourself for tomorrow, or just what you're going through today?" When they came back, I said, "We have to give him an answer. Mr. Phillips has got to have an answer." They told me, "Well, since you got us the jobs here, I guess we'll go along with you." It ended up that we didn't go to the picnic. And the next year they had it so we could go to the picnic with them.

Hind Catchers

"You know when you're playing baseball, the pitcher pitches the ball, and if he barely tips it, the hind catcher has got to catch it or go run and pick it up?"

One of the gentlemen who is retired from the History Department at [Virginia] Tech saw my picture at the last Freedom Fund Dinner, and he must have had it in his office or in his house. He laminated it and sent it to me and said he and his wife were coming to see me. But that's how we met a lot of people at Virginia Tech, because you're always going to have some people like that regardless of how the college feels. You've got all sorts of people, and you're going to always have somebody coming up wanting to see the world better. You have less of those than you do the ones that don't want it. So that's where we met so many people that way.

[Virginia Tech] was the state college, but Blacks couldn't stay on the campus until after integration. We would help them, and then if something happened, I have had them to come here with me just like if a student was staying with you and something happened. You know when you're playing baseball, the pitcher pitches the ball, and if he barely tips it, the hind catcher has got to catch it or go run and pick it up? I always called John and I "hind catchers"—anything that happened that didn't work like it should. Mrs. Ravella Bannister, four or five of us during our young life, we were hind catchers. We would try to pull it up and help.

Students came here and didn't have anywhere to live. We would bring them to our place, then we help them find [places to stay]. But they could not stay on the campus. And the sad part of it was that it was a state college. I could see if it was you and your husband had a private college, but this was a state college. I may not be paying but ten dollars worth of taxes a year, but that's my ten dollars that I owe. But you didn't get the benefit of it.

We have had students here. We had a lot of them. One time I came home and all these girls were here, and wherever they were staying, something happened to the house with the water break. They didn't have anywhere to go. So they slept on the floor here until we found somewhere for them to go.

And a young man was in the paper. He's the head of the Ruritan now, but he's a retired engineer from Hercules. When he came, they couldn't stay in the hotel, and they couldn't stay looking for a job, and they were at the Radford Arsenal, and it was not only them—it was all down through the years. We were just like a hotel reception. When you go in a hotel, you know, and then you don't know whether you want a room or not, a suite or whatever. Well, when you come in this county, you didn't have [anywhere to stay].

You wouldn't believe this. They asked a Black man to come here—now I can't recall where he came from—for a job as the coach. I'm thinking it was the coach of the football team. Who do you think they asked to take him around to show him where people live? John T. Hairston. He was not even on the staff over there. But whoever knew us knew what kind of people we were in the community. Now, wasn't that sad? The man didn't even want the job. But, anyway, that was life.

Chapter 4

COMMUNITY, CIVIL RIGHTS AND POLITICS, 1964–1980

"My husband and I were taught that whenever you moved to or went into a community, you should try and be a part of it."

MAKING THE COMMUNITY BETTER

Almost immediately upon moving to Christiansburg in 1953, John and Nannie Hairston joined the Schaeffer Memorial Baptist Church, the PTA, the NAACP and the Democratic Party. Schaeffer Memorial Baptist Church already had a deep history and iconic place within the community when the Hairstons became members in the mid-1950s. Captain Charles S. Schaeffer, who founded the Christiansburg Institute, also founded the church, which started out as the Christiansburg African Baptist Church in 1867.[22] Schaeffer later deeded the property to the board of trustees, most of whom were formerly enslaved, and became the pastor from 1879 until his death in 1899. During that time, the name of the church was changed to Memorial Baptist Church. It was changed again in the 1940s to the current Schaeffer Memorial Baptist Church. The building was built in 1885 at the same time that the Christiansburg Institute Building (Hill School) was built next door.[23] Both the Schaeffer Memorial Baptist Church and the Christiansburg Institute Building are listed in the Virginia Landmarks Register (1978) and the National Register of Historic Places (1979). Schaeffer also procured land to be used for a cemetery for the

Hill School and Schaeffer Memorial Baptist Church. *Montgomery Museum.*

former enslaved on the outskirts of town, which is another part of his legacy to the African American community.

The Hill School closed in 1953 when the new Friends Elementary School, which was built for African American students, opened. In 1967, it reopened as the Christiansburg Community Center. John and Nannie were very involved in the development and operation of the Center, which included Head Start, youth recreation and classes in Black history. The preservation of the Hill School was a major focus of Nannie's life.

When the Hairstons arrived in Christiansburg in the mid-1950s, their two school-age daughters attended segregated schools. Catherine and Edwina went first to Friends Elementary, when it opened in 1953 for elementary African American students, and later to Christiansburg Institute. The landmark case by the U.S. Supreme Court that struck down segregated schools in America, *Brown v. Board of Education*, was decided in May 1954. However, Virginia's state government adopted the policy of massive resistance that prevented desegregation in some cases until the 1970s. It wasn't until the school year of 1966–67 that Christiansburg High School was integrated.

Nannie talks about being a homeroom parent and member of the strong PTA at Friends Elementary that fought for new books, better supplies and a piano for the school's use. An early battle in the Hairstons' tenure with the PTA was a case involving Reverend Archie Richmond. Richmond was the head teacher at Friends Elementary and also the minister of the St.

Captain Charles Schaeffer and the First African Baptist Church's Board of Deacons, undated. *Smokehouse Collection, Christiansburg Institute Museum & Archives.*

Paul AME Church in Blacksburg, Virginia. In August 1955, he was with members of his church for a picnic at a park in nearby Wythe County when he refused to take his congregation to the Black section of the park. He was arrested, and although he was later acquitted, the superintendent of schools in Montgomery County tried to fire him from his position at Friends Elementary. Black citizens, including the PTA at Friends Elementary, were instrumental in his maintaining his job.[24]

Reverend Richmond, in tandem with other ministers in Blacksburg, is credited with founding the Virginia Council on Human Relations in the area soon after this event. The Council on Human Relations was an interracial, national organization that emerged as a response to the civil unrest of the 1950s and 1960s to promote school desegregation and fair employment practices and improve relations between Blacks and Whites. John and Nannie Hairston joined the Council on Human Relations and trained with them. Nannie Hairston credits the organization with helping to keep the peace and desegregating without violence in Southwest Virginia.

John and Nannie Hairston
with Andrew Young, May
1970. *Hairston family.*

The Hairstons also joined a strong core of older African Americans who were members of the local chapter of the NAACP (Montgomery County–Radford City–Floyd County Branch 7092), including Samuel H. Clark, Reverend George and Mattie Calloway, Nathan and Verna Holmes and Ed Reynolds. Each member took turns at office holding and paid the dues for the branch to remain a voting member in the national conference. They were members all their lives and held major leadership positions.

The Hairstons also joined the Montgomery County Democratic Party soon after arriving in the county. Their involvement and influence developed over time. In the 1970s, Nannie was one of the most committed foot soldiers for electing and reelecting State Senator Madison Marye. John was elected delegate for Montgomery County to attend the national Democratic convention in the 1970s. In 1980, Nannie was elected as an alternate delegate at large from the 9th Congressional District and in 1988 was elected as delegate. The next decade saw their standing in the local Democratic Party and, indeed, at the state and national level soar to new heights.

In 1969, John's philanthropy and nonprofit work expanded when he helped form the Christiansburg Housing Corporation, a nonprofit designed to build housing for the poor. The organization trained and hired unskilled and handicapped local citizens and worked with Virginia Polytechnic Institute (Virginia Tech) Architecture Department. He was recognized for this work in 1972 when he was invited to the Kennedy Center in Washington, D.C., and honored as one of America's outstanding volunteers.[25]

John also established the first Health Systems Agency in Southwest Virginia and served as its first president from 1976 to 1980. The organization, with its

John and Nannie
Hairston, with
Elaine and
Albert Reed.
Hairston family.

large staff of volunteers, did research and promoted ideas to clinics, hospitals and nursing homes that led to better healthcare in the region.

At the same time that the Hairstons' community involvement was increasing, Nannie was also contributing to the local community through her employment at the Radford Army Ammunition Plant. She was hired in 1963 in the custodial department, at the time the only opportunity for an African American woman at the plant, and about ten years later moved into production. While there, she helped promote African American history through corporate-sponsored Black History Month activities, and she was a proud union member (Local No. 3-495 Oil, Chemical and Atomic Workers International Union).

SCHAEFFER MEMORIAL BAPTIST CHURCH

"It's a beautiful history behind that church."

I was pregnant with my third daughter, Dy-Anne Marie Hairston, when we moved to Christiansburg in July [1953]. Dy-Anne was born in September, so I think I had been here just about two weeks, and I decided that I was going to join the church before the baby was born, and I did. I actually joined the church before my husband. He was working away from the job he had when

Schaeffer Memorial Baptist Church. *Montgomery Museum.*

he started working here. He actually started at Radford Army Ammunition Plant, and he wasn't satisfied with that. But in the meantime, he had a lot of things that he had to get straightened out and done, so I just decided that I would go on and join. And just moving into Christiansburg and then buying this home, we had a lot of things to take care of. I joined the church two to three weeks after I came here. Before the end of August, I was at Schaeffer Memorial Baptist Church.

That was the faith that I believed in and had been all my life, so I didn't go in the community trying to find out or in the county about another church. It was close. I didn't really ask anyone any more than: Where is the church that most of the Baptist people go here in Montgomery County? And they told me. So I picked that church, and I'm very happy that I did, because the church has such a long history.

Captain Schaeffer built the church in 1885 and bought eleven acres of land for [former] slaves to be buried on Radford Road. We are using that land today. My husband and my parents are buried there. That land has a history. And so it was just a wonderful experience. When you think about integration—when I came here, a Caucasian lady was playing the piano in 1953 for Schaeffer, and it was founded by the Quakers sending Captain Schaeffer here for the [former] slaves, so it's a beautiful history behind that church.

The church was named Memorial Baptist Church, and Reverend [Fleming Emory] Alexander decided that it should be named after Captain Schaeffer, so that's when the name Schaeffer Memorial Baptist Church came into being [in the 1940s].[26] Also, I mentioned the cemetery that we have on Radford Road, which is eleven acres of land, Captain Schaeffer purchased through someone else. After he found out that he couldn't buy the material and they wouldn't sell the eleven acres because he made a statement that he wanted to bury the slaves, someone [bought the land for him]. In the consecrated book, it doesn't tell the name of the person that purchased the land for Captain Schaeffer.[27]

As a West Virginia person coming to Montgomery County in 1953, I was so thrilled to come to a community where there was a church, a fresh building that was erected for a school, and come to found out eleven acres of land that was still here, and we are still burying in that place. It's over half full. But out of all of the things that we saw in the community, my husband and I could see a lot of things that needed to be done, and we wanted to make ourselves available. My reason and my husband's reason [for that was] we were taught wherever we moved to or went into a community, you should try to be a part of it.

Friends Elementary School

"That's what makes your community better,
when we can step over the line and do for others."

During those years, we didn't have the facilities. And the grade school—when I came here, we were getting books that came from the White school. They were handed over to the Friends Elementary School and how I got to know it, and it's a fact, and not what somebody told me.

I had three nieces that came here and spent a year with us, and one day—[one of them] was a very little girl at the time, but she was very smart—and I said, "Mae Frances, it's time for you to go and get your homework." And she said, "Aunt Nannie Mae, I don't have to. We had the same book last year." I said, "What?" And that's when I started going to the schools, and finally we got organized as a PTA, and we learned a lot of things that we could do to help ourselves.

Reverend [Archie] Richmond, who was the principal for my older girl [Catherine] when she was in school—I don't know if you were at that dinner when he mentioned about the park he went in. He told us about going to the park and they asked him to move, and he refused. Then they carried him to jail, but they released him, and then they wanted to take his school away from him. Anyway, Irene Green and Cora Peck, she's in the nursing home over here behind me now. We went through the community getting names, and we got over a couple hundred names of people requesting not to get rid of Mr. Richmond, and we felt like that was the beginning of some things that we started doing before we even got our PTA and all that going like we had in the next year or so. We actually took it to the school board to keep Mr. Richmond here. And they listened to us, and he stayed here until he got ready to retire from here.

So we started going to the school board and finally found out some things that we needed to change, and we started doing things for ourselves through the PTA. Actually, I was a homeroom mother. That means if you're a homeroom mother, and something happened at school, and the principal feels that he needs to have some advice or someone to help, they would call you if you were a homeroom mother. And if I was available, I would go down and see what I could do, if I could help with whatever their problem was. I was a homeroom mother for two or three years.

The biggest thing you would do is working with your PTA. For instance, we bought our own piano at the Friends Elementary School. We had a queen

Friends Elementary School, March 1963. *Gladys Sokolow Collection, Christiansburg Institute Museum & Archives.*

rally, and that's how we got our piano for our auditorium. The school board didn't give us one. So we bought one. We had a queen contest, and that's how we got the money. The only thing we knew was we didn't have decent books, so you know we weren't going to have a piano.

I've always belonged to the PTA regardless, all the way down through my children's lives. Whatever organization or anything that parents should be involved in, John and I have always joined—not only for our children—but for any child that we felt like where the parents didn't get too much involved in it. That's what makes your community better, when we can step over the line and do for others.

NATIONAL ASSOCIATION FOR THE ADVANCEMENT OF COLORED PEOPLE

"We say all people."

It doesn't matter how poor you are or how rich you are, this organization can help motivate any person in the community according to the rules and regulations. They're for anyone and the things that happen with discrimination—you don't have to have money. That's the most beautiful part of this organization. Really, you don't have to be a paying member. If you need help, and I'm sure you understand what I'm getting ready to say. When they say a "Freedom Fund Dinner," we have money raised, and when someone has to be helped and they don't have money, we still can operate, because it doesn't matter whether you're Black or White.

Back in the early '60s, the organization didn't have Whites in this community with it, but eventually, between 1960 and 1970, I have pictures to show you where we had a Freedom Fund Dinner and we started inviting the mayors and our congressmen. We've had governors to come speak to us. And that has created a better relationship. The reason some places have so much trouble in their community, between their community and your government, local or state, is because you don't have any relationship. You don't know what I'm all about, and they don't know what you are about.

And so when you have a Freedom Fund Dinner, if you can step out and start inviting low-income people, regardless—just invite them. Just because you don't have an education or money, you can't keep that person from getting involved. They could be one of the most gifted persons that can help motivate your organization than someone who is a student in college or a professor at a college. So what I like about it, it's meant for all people.

When the NAACP was created in 1909 in New York, and this White person—I don't know if I've given you the names of them. I can get you a small brochure that I have, if you make a note and remind me of it, when it was organized in New York. We have people today, not only Whites or Blacks, think that it's just for Black people. But no. We say all people. And if you really think about it, when they say color, and I try to illustrate it down through the years when I was out able to work and trying to get members, I made this illustration and have kept it in my mind, and it worked.

I belong to the Eastern Star, and you have to wear all white, you know, gloves. That's our uniform. We wear white dresses, white shoes, white stockings when we go to a meeting. That's just like your school colors. That's just the colors of it. And the Masons usually wear black suits, white shirts and black ties. I was going to the store and thought about it one day. I was going to buy a dress. So once I had tried to get someone to join the NAACP, and I think they were Caucasian. I'm almost sure it was. And he or she, whoever it was, some years and years ago, said, "Oh, I thought that was just for colored people." I said, "It says colored people, but I just went to the store to buy a dress for the Eastern Star." They said, "What kind of dress?" I said, "Just a dress that you would wear, not a formal, because I belong to an organization that we have basic colors." You could wear a white uniform, but most of us try to find a dress that's kind of dressy-like. "And I would like to have it in white."

So I told this person I was talking to, a Caucasian, "If that dress is bought in white, what other color could I put in place of white? No color, because white has red, blue and all colors." I'm trying to show you where it says the National Association for the Advancement of Colored People. Then I repeat that it was organized in 1909, and I can't think of her name now, but I have it on paper [Mary White Ovington]. It was organized starting with a Caucasian lady. That should tell the world something.

We had a strong group. It wasn't too many of us, but when we came here, John and I met these strong Afro-American people trying to hold

Nannie Hairston, on far right. *Hairston family.*

this organization together, and it just kept on. I've been in it ever since I've been living in Christiansburg, sixty-some years. I can name them all. Mr. Samuel H. Clark. Our secretary was Mattie Calloway. She was the secretary for twenty-five years. Her husband was Reverend George Calloway. They were just like John and I, working together. They did it up until they died. She lived until she was one hundred, I think. Ed Reynolds, and you may have met Rita Holmes [Irvin]—she's Afro-American, retired from the school system, and she's working in different programs here. Her father, Nathan Holmes—I've got pictures of him and his wife, Verna, and brother Zimri and Rosa Holmes. He was one of the backbones keeping this organization together.

You have to pay an assessment. You have to maintain fifty people to have a charter. We didn't have enough money to pay our assessment, and when we came here, it was $400, and that was a lot of money during those days. So John mentioned, "Well, why would we want to go to the convention and not vote?" And two or three more agreed, and I agreed with it solely because we talked. Why would you want to go to the convention in wherever it is in the state of Virginia? You can't vote, because if you don't pay your assessment, you can't vote, which makes sense. So we'd get together and pay the assessment—the few people that we had. It wasn't a crowd.

I didn't realize at one time I was a treasurer until I read something in one of these books that I've just picked up. I said, "Oh my gosh, I was a treasurer of it." If you were on a committee, three, five or seven, and you couldn't come up with anyone, we just had three or four of us. We'd just take that position and hold it until you find [someone]. And that's the only way you can keep an organization going.

Montgomery County Democratic Party

"Don't ever let anyone tell you one vote doesn't matter. It does."

A Good Foundation

My daddy couldn't read or write, and he voted. Didn't I mention that to you? Say this coming Wednesday it's going to be Election Day, and this weekend, you've got a sample ballot out. One person would take that ballot and show my daddy [and say], "Are you voting Republican or Democrat?"

And he would tell you what he's voting. You'd show it to him, that was it. And if you go to Blacksburg at the library, you'll see a room dedicated to Mary Fessler. I had to work, and John had gotten in this accident, and he couldn't take my father, because he couldn't drive on account of his back, and we had to get somebody to carry Mama and Daddy to the poll. Mrs. Fessler heard me talking, and she said, "You don't have anything to worry about." They were retired from Virginia Tech, and it amazed her. We told her the story because she was a good friend of ours. We were all working on the Council on Human Relations to make our community better. So we got to know them. She said, "We'll be happy to take your parents." And they were so enthused. They could not believe—my mother could read and write—here's people going to vote. One went to the fourth grade, and the other one [didn't go to school]. And we never had to tell him. He was anxious to go and to vote.

That's why I don't have sympathy when you run into people and they say, "I don't vote." I say, "Well, why? Look how long we fought to get this privilege, and then you don't want to take it, and you have the ability to know whose name is who." I don't go through a whole story like with you, but I tell them, "I know of people, they can't read or write, and they learned who the candidates are. And if your mind and your brain can function, you can program it," I said, "just like a computer." My daddy and mother voted until they got where they couldn't.

Years ago, all colored people were thinking that they had to vote Republican because of Abraham Lincoln. That was the big deal until they really found out. These are the words I heard my mother say. That's why I can remember Mr. Roosevelt. She told my aunt, she said, "Irene, I'm going to change my vote. It can't get any worse. I'm going to vote for Mr. Roosevelt." And she [continued], "Now, what you're going to do, I don't know." [Her sister Irene] said, "Well, Bessie, we've been doing things together."

Delegates

We joined [the Montgomery Count Democratic Party] John and I. John went to the meeting before I did. I think I told you about John going to a Democratic meeting in the courthouse. That's where they met when we first came here. John said, "Sugar, here's another meeting, and I'm about to meet—and look at the time." John never liked to go to anything late. I'd be sitting there talking and he would say, "Now, Nan, aren't you supposed to go to a meeting?" I'd say, "Yes." "Well, it's time for you to get ready and get out of here. And put your brains in gear before you open your mouth." But he went to that meeting, and Senator [Madison] Marye said, "Here this great big tall man came through the door." My husband was six foot and five and a half inches tall. They could hear somebody coming down, wherever they were meeting, John found out, because at that time we didn't have an elevator. It wasn't like it is now.

But anyway, John said he got there and he sat down. He kept waiting on maybe one or two more Blacks to come, and nobody showed up. Well, John went through that when he introduced himself. And the next year, sweetheart, or maybe the next two years, John put his name in for a delegate for the Democratic Party, and don't ask me because I don't know whether it was in New York or Florida the first time we ever went to a convention.

At that meeting, John said, "I would like to go to the convention, but I wouldn't want someone to nominate me just because I'm Black." Someone had asked him if he would like to be on it, and that's what made him get up to speak. It was a White woman, and she said, "I'm from Grundy, and I have always wanted to do something for a colored person," because they weren't calling us Black then. And she said, "I would like to nominate John T. Hairston." Then, before they went through the motion with it, John asked for the floor. He said, "Don't nominate me or vote for me because I'm colored." Because we still were using "colored" ourselves. "I would like to go to represent Montgomery County Democrats." And he got elected. He called me, and said, "Well, you can start [packing]. I was elected as a delegate to go to the convention." That was our beginning, getting involved, really. And from that day on we stayed with them, and still, up until it got where we couldn't go.

Out in the Cold

A woman, who was in the House of Delegates, her parents had a restaurant in Blacksburg.[28] I think I told you the story about how Colette would go with me to put out materials for Senator Marye, which he just retired. It was a cold rain, and then it stopped raining like it's doing out there now. But it wasn't a whole lot of rain, just come and go. But it was real cold, and we'd been out all that week. This must have been on a Friday. It must have been the end of the week, because Colette said, "Mother, I'm hungry." I said, "We're going to give out on this street and then we're going home." So I decided, I said, "Well, maybe I'll buy some soup and just take it home." And she said, "I'm hungry." [Colette] was twelve or thirteen.

I went and [was told], "You know, we can't serve you." But she told us that we could go on the other side, because it's almost closing time, where nobody would see us, and eat the soup, and that's what happened. Then Colette asked me, "Now, Mother, do you have to pay for me when you take me to the doctor or will Senator Marye pay for it? You shouldn't have to pay it."

COUNCIL ON HUMAN RELATIONS

"You didn't have to go to Alabama to find a place you can't eat."

The same thing was happening across the country. It happened right here. You didn't have to go to Alabama to find a place you can't eat, or North Carolina. They're still talking about what happened to people when they'd try to have sit-ins. But we didn't try to have sit-ins. As I said, my husband and I worked on the Council on Human Relations. We'd just go after we were trained how to go and apply for a job or either go and try to eat, but you have to mind your language you use and walk back out and say, "Thank you." We created a very nice atmosphere here. We still didn't have a problem, like fighting. You may not like when somebody tells you they didn't want to feed you, but we would ask the question, "If integration [does] come, how are you going to accept it?" Some answered you, and most of them didn't answer you. And I can understand that.

We didn't march. John and I, we asked people. It being a small area, you didn't have too many people really within the NAACP. But we were training. We were on the Council on Human Relations, and we joined with them. We would talk with some people who came down from New York, and I don't know where the others were from. And to teach you, if you didn't know how to respond, if you call me out by my name, tell me I can't sit there, we'd just get up and leave. We went through that with three or four [local establishments].

When you're out doing volunteer work, or like we've been with the NAACP all our life, just about, working, with that kind of organization, some people don't know what it means, and they want to make like we are all Ku Klux Klansmen—we are all on the hate side. No. But you have to learn how to control yourself. Everybody can't be a good volunteer worker for certain organizations when they're going out to try to better a community.

You have to know how. Sometimes you have to take things you don't want to take, you have to speak things that you have to say behind closed doors. You can't say it in public.

RADFORD ARMY AMMUNITION PLANT

"At that time, when I went there, you worked in roads and grounds, custodian, and that was it."

As I told you, when I went to Hercules [Radford Army Ammunition Plant], there was a sign on the bathroom door, "Whites Only," and I'm starting in the bathroom. I didn't even look at a sign. And they said, "Uh-oh." The lady from England said, "Love, you go over there and they have a stall over there for colored."

And the men that worked on roads and grounds rode one bus. Now, they were going down there to cut grass together, and another bus carried the Black men. And then there was one Black man on the bus, and my husband, he rode that for three or four weeks. And John said, "There's a White man riding our bus, and I can't understand." So John finally got enough nerve to ask somebody. They said, "No, he's colored." He had enough colored blood in him to be classified as an Afro-American or colored man, whichever way they did it. That's the way it was. He became one of our best friends. He was a minister and his name was Elder Lewis. At that time, when I went there, you worked in roads and grounds, custodian, and that was it.

When I went to work at Hercules, and for two weeks, Stella Grubb was off ill, and John had tried to get me a job. And the lady's name that you just read, Gustava Carter, was one of the Black women that was at Schaeffer Church serving, and she worked for Congressman [Richard Harding] Poff's mother. That family still owns a lot of property here now. She said, "Why are you trying to get ahold of Congressman Poff?" He said, "Well, if you want to know anything, get anything, you go to the heads of your government." She said, "Well, I know where he is. He's up here at Claytor Lake. I used to take care of him when he was a baby. I used to work for his mother." That's how we got ahold of him. He gave a name to John to get in touch with; and I might get hired. And that's how I found out that, if this girl, whenever she came back, that was the only opening they had, as the janitor. I would have to leave.

Well, orders came down from Washington before my two weeks was up to hire Negroes or colored people into production. They were not working in production then, and you had Whites that didn't know how to read. We had foremen who couldn't read. And he was sweet as he could be, my foreman, when I was in there as janitor. If I'd go over and say, "I want off tomorrow at twelve o' clock. I need to go home. I need to take care of some things." He'd say, "Go over and get your time card and clock out." Well, you're going to get off at twelve, between eleven-thirty and twelve you get to the office, you just reach up there and get your card and hand it to him. That's the way it was in some areas. I'm just showing you how we were treated. And you still had to go along and carry a smile on your face, and I'm just glad I was taught not to hate.

This White guy asked me one day, "Hairston, you know you all are going to be able to go in the new cafeteria," when they made a new cafeteria. My number was 15408. It was on the back of the overalls that we wore. Sometimes they called me Hairston and sometimes 15408. Things began to change. This was an order that came down from the government in the early 1960s.

I worked in there for a good little while before they put us in production. The people that were in the Janitor Department, I was told by my foreman and supervisor, "If any of these choose to go in production when we tell them, then we have an opening, and you can stay." I stayed there twenty years, ten years in production and ten years in custodian [work].

I belonged to the union [Local No. 3-495 Oil, Chemical and Atomic Workers International Union]. We had a union so when something went wrong we could go to the union, when Hercules, we felt like, had done us wrong. It wasn't that Hercules had the union. And when you go to Fairlawn, it's still there, the building where they still have a union. And if people want to join it, you join it. And that would upset me, but I wouldn't let them know it. Like you'd be sitting there, and we'd been in a meeting with the company, and they'd say, "Are we getting a raise?" But see, they didn't want to join the union to pay dues. They were going to get the same raise that I'm getting, but we were out there fighting for it.

I look at my parents. I came up under a union. I remember when my father used to have to go to work before the sun came up, they were in the mines and when they came out of the mines, the sun had gone down. And when President Roosevelt came in, the New Deal came in. That's when things changed for people to work an eight-hour shift. And these are the things I can recall as a young child. A lot of people in this life don't really realize what a blessing they have, and if they hear the story, then maybe they would appreciate life more and would really appreciate people more than they actually do. Not so much businesspeople. Ordinary people you meet that have gone through things to make things better for us.

And that's one thing that I try to teach my children. John and I tried to tell people in this life, whether you're White or Black, you have to learn to respect people. And out of respect, you can get a lot of things that you normally wouldn't get, if you knew how to be a respectable person. Have you seen people, and somebody says, "Wonder how they can get this and that?" It's the way they carried themselves, the way they treated people. My parents taught us: Learn to respect people that respect you, and that keeps it going.

Chapter 5

A SEAT AT THE TABLE, 1980–2017

*"You've got to have a way of knowing how to address yourself
to people to get something done."*

CREATING THE CONVERSATION, TAKING THEIR RIGHTFUL SEAT AND BUILDING THE TABLE

In Nannie's archive, there is a copy of the letter dated May 6, 1980, addressed to "Fellow Democrats" in which she is seeking election as a delegate at large from the 9th Congressional District to represent the district at the national convention that year. In the letter, she lays out her qualifications: Schaeffer Memorial Baptist Church vice-president of the Deaconess Board; League of Women Voters (she was a founding member); St. John Chapter 80 Eastern Star; state co-advisor, Youth & College Division Virginia State Conference National Association for the Advancement of Colored People; Christiansburg United Way Board of Directors; New River Valley Historical Society; member, Political Action Committee, Local No. 3-495 Oil, Chemical and Atomic Workers International Union; and employee, Radford Army Ammunition Plant. She also stated that she had been an active member of the Montgomery County Democratic Party for twenty-six years. This list of achievements details the remarkable place Nannie B. Hairston found herself in 1980—fifty-nine years old, working full time with a family, having struggled for equality from the society at large and yet making such a difference in the world.

By 1980, she and John had surely made a place for themselves not only in the African American community in Christiansburg but also in the community at large and in local, state and national organizations. The Hairstons were both lifetime members of the NAACP, and they both held executive positions in their local branch. The Montgomery County–Radford City–Floyd County Branch no. 7092 had been an important part of their community involvement since arriving in the area. John served as the branch's president from 1983 to 1989. Nannie served as membership chair for more than twenty years and as treasurer and worked with the NAACP Youth Council. In addition, both she and John served on the state NAACP board for ten years or more.

Nannie Hairston helped organize the annual Freedom Fund Banquet, which began in 1975. It was her vision to create a framework for people of all denominations to come together. By 1990, the guest list included Whites, Blacks, Republicans, Democrats, local officeholders, business people and NAACP members and non-members, and it became a very successful fundraising vehicle. At its height, it was held at Virginia Tech with at least five hundred in attendance with a nationally known speaker and dignitaries in attendance.

In 1991, she was the first recipient of the Nannie B. Hairston Community Service Award. The award has now been given to more than thirty individuals

Left: NAACP Freedom Fund Banquet. Nannie Hairston and Lindsay West, winner of the Nannie B. Hairston Service Award, 2011. *James Klagge*.

Opposite: Coretta Scott King and Nannie Hairston with other unidentified individuals, circa 1980s. *Hairston family*.

who have shown exceptional service to the community, many of whom Nannie worked with to make the community better. Recipients included Lindsay West, Reverend Archie L. Richmond, Lois Teele and Dr. Nathaniel L. Bishop. Fittingly, John Hairston was honored with the award named for his wife in 2001.

She and John were also very involved in local Democratic Party politics and became powerful figures whose votes and influence were sought after by candidates for mayor, the House of Delegates and the State Senate, governor, U.S. senator and even U.S. president. John was delegate to the national convention twice, and Nannie was a delegate in 1988 and an alternate delegate in 1980. They were members of the National Black Caucus, an organization that included national figures such as Julian Bond, Andrew Young and Coretta Scott King. Nannie Hairston was also, importantly, one of the Montgomery County campaign managers for Jesse Jackson when he ran for president in 1984 and in 1988.

The Hairstons were supporters and friends of Douglas Wilder. Wilder was a Virginia state senator from 1976 to 1986 and the first African American governor in Virginia (1990–94). In fact, Wilder was the first African American governor elected to any U.S. state since Reconstruction. They met him at a Democratic Party meeting in Richmond sometime in the late 1970s, invited him to be the keynote speaker for the NAACP Freedom Fund Banquet in

June 1976 and developed a deep friendship. The Hairstons, family members and friends attended his inauguration as governor in 1990, as well as the Inaugural Ball in their own box.

Even though neither ever held elected office, they were pivotal in Democratic Party politics. They developed a strong bond with local state senator Madison Marye. Not only did they campaign for Marye, but they also became lifelong friends with the senator and his wife. Candidates for senator and governor made their way to Montgomery County for private meetings and public events to gain the Hairstons' imprimatur and secure votes from Southwest Virginia. Dr. Nathaniel L. Bishop remembers being introduced to Gordon Baliles, the sixty-fifth governor of Virginia (1986–90), when he was running for governor at a meeting the Hairstons suggested he attend.[29] When I was going through the boxes of Mrs. Hairston's archive, I ran across many cards and letters from Democratic officials and politicians and a Christmas card from Senator Mark Warner and his family every year. In addition, Senator Warner gave an impassioned virtual introduction to my talk, "The Life and Legacy of Nannie B. Hairston," at the Montgomery-Floyd Regional Library in 2018, calling her a "civil rights advocate who made a huge difference in his life and in the Commonwealth of Virginia."[30]

Nannie Hairston and Bessie Berger, mid-1980s. *Hairston family.*

Nannie Hairston and Mark Warner.
Hairston family.

But as I understand it, it was not just Democratic politicians who made the pilgrimage to the Hairstons' door. In 2018, former delegate Nick Rush (7th District) remembered meeting with the Hairstons as a twenty-three-year-old Republican FedEx driver who was running for the board of supervisors in Montgomery County, and he remembered their encouragement and support.[31] By the time Rush retired in 2022, he had served in political office for twenty-five years.

The Hairstons did indeed provide supportive, advisory and crucial roles for officeholders, politicians and fellow activists. But their reach was broader and deeper than that. Nan and John Hairston provided a table that was long enough and wide enough to include Democrats and Republicans, landowners and homeless, White and Black, business people and workers—in other words, all people from the region and beyond. They brought people together to try and solve problems and keep the peace, and in so doing they formed an all-inclusive—ecumenical, if you will—community to sit at the table and at their table.

Fiftieth Wedding Anniversary Party

*"At one time, we couldn't go there. Now, we can go,
so why am I going to a hotel?"*

That's where we had it, over at [Virginia] Tech, where we're having everything at the Inn [at Virginia Tech and Skelton Conference Center] now. But it used to be Donaldson Brown. So we had our anniversary there [in 1991]. It was just a marvelous dinner.

One of my oldest daughter's friends spent most of his time in Africa with his job, at least six months out of a year. So he looked at the map and saw how small Christiansburg is, and he was saying "Donaldson Brown Center."

Above: Nannie and John Hairston at their fiftieth wedding anniversary party, Donaldson Brown Conference Center, Virginia Tech, 1991. *Hairston family*.

Opposite: Benjamin T. Penn, Nannie Hairston, James B. McDaniel, at the Donaldson Brown Conference Center, Virginia Tech, 1991. *Hairston family*.

He didn't say anything about the college. That's what was on the invitation. But we had somebody at each hotel to be there because we had about three hotels. We had them at each hotel, so when they got ready to go to Virginia Tech, they wouldn't get lost and go on a country road and we'd be looking for them. This same gentleman told us the next morning, "I have never been so surprised. When we got to the Donaldson Brown Center, here these White young men walk out with black suits on, white shirts, and the bowtie, opened up our door, and the door to go back into Donaldson Brown to go into the college. Someone opened the door up there." He says, "Is this happening in Virginia? I can't believe this."

The reason we had it [at Virginia Tech], I don't think I told you. They had just built the Marriott—and my girls said, "Mother, why don't we go and look at the Marriott and have it there?" I said, "I don't think I would like to have it there." They said, "Why?" I said, "You know what? Virginia Tech is a state school, and still." I said, "And Catherine, you lived five miles from Virginia Tech, and when you graduated, you couldn't go there because

it was a predominantly White college. But yet, it was a state school. We had to send you to down by Richmond, in that area, to an all-Black college [Virginia State University]." She said, "Well, that was then, Mother." I said, "I know it. Now, we can go to Virginia Tech." I have a letter in my folder where they thanked me for having our fiftieth anniversary at Virginia Tech. But that was my reason for having it there. At one time, we couldn't go there. Now, we can go, so why am I going to a hotel? That's what actually started us having NAACP dinners there.

We had a lot of relationships from that day on that we made ourselves. [For example], you may hear about a play and think, "Boy, wouldn't I like to see that?" But we couldn't go. Some White person had to buy a ticket and we had to go with you. Now, these are the kinds of things [we went through]. Then I used to have friends that would tell me, "Why would you want to go somewhere where you're not wanted?" I said, "Then I'm going to miss this play. So I'm just going to ignore them."

Actually, Mr. Frank Bannister worked for three or four presidents of Virginia Tech as a butler. We'd go over, like the play is going to be this evening. His wife would take him over to Burruss Hall. That's where it was. She would take him over to Burruss Hall, and he would park his truck there and she'd take him back home. Then when John and I leave here, we'd go up to Blacksburg and pick her up, and Mr. Bannister. And if he wasn't going—most likely he didn't—he would move the truck and everybody never did know. When we came out of Burruss Hall and came down those steps and the next flight of steps, we were right there—it could be in the wintertime, cold, raining, we never got that wet. That's where we always parked.

I'm just saying, these are some experiences I've had right here in the county. All of that was brought about telling you about our anniversary. That's why I wanted to have the party at Virginia Tech, because we weren't allowed to go there unless we were mowing the grass or working in one of their dormitories, cleaning, or either in the kitchen cooking.

Breaking the Color Barrier

"Your mouth can sometimes do more harm than a pistol."

I was going down the hallway at Hercules, and I really can't call his name, but Dr. [D.B.] Jurisson was my dentist, and this was his son-in-law, and I said, "Why are you walking and talking and at the same time walking backwards?" He said, "I've got to go and get to the [meeting]." He was an engineer, and I was a janitor. He said, "I've got to go to a United Way meeting, and I've got to get some things done here in the office before I go." And he said, "Why don't you join the United Way?" I said, "Are you going home this evening?" He said, "Yes." I said, "Well, could I ride in your car without asking you?" And he looked at me. I said, "In other words, if you want me to join the United Way, you need to [ask me]." He said, "There's an opening." Somebody had either retired or quit.

I said, "Well, why don't you take my name in? How can I join it without somebody making the first step for me?" So he carried my name in, and they voted on me, and I think I showed you a picture. Dr. Oscar Williams was the second [African American board member]. When I came off the board, I turned his name in, and he was voted in. But he didn't stay long. He didn't even stay a year. He said, "I've got too much going on over here at Virginia Tech, and trying to do things in the community, and I don't think I can deal with these people."

One of the gentlemen [on the board] told my husband—I don't know where John was at, some type of meeting—he said, "You've got a strong wife. I don't see how she goes through what she goes through when she asks for things for the [Christiansburg] Community Center." And you knew everybody around that table didn't like you. You know what I mean? It's not as if they really would talk about doing harm to you, but your mouth can do more harm sometimes than a pistol.

But I went right there with them, and I'd be trying to tell them where we need money for the community, especially the Black community. But I made it through and accumulated a lot of relationships that wouldn't have been without the United Way. You know, somebody has got to stick with them. That's the only way you are ever going to get anywhere. If there's something you want to achieve, you had to learn to stick with it.

Youth Council

"You have to look at the rest of your life."

John and I came in the community and found out that there was just so much need for members of the [NAACP] organization. I tried to teach young people when I was at the [Christiansburg Community] Center or with a group of young people, especially Afro-American young men and women. I would tell my granddaughter, just like our sisters when they go to college, they want to join the sorority group. You're going to pay three or four hundred to join. I said there's nothing wrong with that, but while you're there you could organize a Youth Department on campus of the NAACP. I said a sorority cannot go to a courtroom and argue for your case if you get in trouble.

Something happens to you, fraternities, these young men, you need to learn that it's fine, there's nothing wrong with joining that, but the NAACP is going to the bat for you. So you must realize it's nice doing something that you're going to have a good time and a nice time, but you have to look at the rest of your life. You've got to have something to back you up. You don't want to get into trouble. You may be able to help someone else. And it isn't always trouble. It's trying to find a resource to make your life better, and it is one of the nicest organizations to belong to.

We just started working with them [when we came here in 1953], and regardless of whatever happened, like I've told you, within the NAACP and with the Community Center, if something had to be paid to keep it going, we had two or three of us, sometimes four, more, at least five. We'd come together and give whatever had to be done, and this is before we ever were able to get money from the community. I'm saying that, when you get on the board, some boards you don't get on unless you have money [in the bank] or property. They ask you to be on the board because they expect you to do things, not only just to vote, but when it comes necessary for money, to be able to put forth that money. I learned that when I first went on the [NAACP] state board. I was on the state [board] for ten years, and John was on the state [board] for ten to twelve years.

That's in Richmond. But normally you don't get on the board unless you have a certain amount of property or something. You have to have some kind of real estate or means, if the board gets in trouble. The reason I'm saying that to you, I got up one morning and told my husband—there was a board meeting that day: "I don't think I feel like going to the board meeting today." He said, "Oh, yes, you're going to go today." Because he said he didn't feel like driving, he said, "We'll find somebody to help you and drive you, or help you drive." Because we had a situation in Mississippi that needed to be addressed, and it needed money, and, see, they know we own property, because that all had been put into the [record] when I went in as a board member. You can't have a board that needs something without people having means.

So he just wanted to make sure I'm there to know what's going on so we know what to expect, because if they needed money, we knew the situation. I never had to go into anything. We always had something come up to address the issue, and we got through it. But still, you had to go to those meetings. You don't wait on them to send you a letter to tell you what happened in the business meeting. But he knew that it was possible something could come up if they had a situation on their hands to address.

We have given it, but we never had to give up all we had, so it's been a pleasure of working and seeing something advance. It could have gone down, but we had strong people, and that's why it's hard for us now to see people so inactive. They seem like they don't care whether you have an NAACP when you talk with them. But if they get in trouble, they know who to address.

It's always in the newsletter, whatever comes up, and that's how you keep up. And see, we have a state office in Richmond. Mr. Jack Gravely is acting now, because the president that we had for years is not there anymore, and they just don't go out and get someone. They have to have a committee to seek out and find another president. But if anything happens, say in Roanoke, and we want to address it, what we really should do is to contact our state office, and they tell you. Then, if no one there can tell you or you cannot reach anyone, then your next move is to your national. And whenever the state can't answer your question, they go to the national.

They tell you whether they need you or whether you should go or what you should do. But we have our guidance with the state office. And whoever represents this area, and if we had an NAACP in Pulaski and Wytheville—we go as far as the Tennessee line for Virginia, and that person is over Wytheville, Tennessee, Pulaski, back to Montgomery County. Roanoke is in another district, and they go down on back to Charlottesville. But if you have questions that you need to know how to address, then you call, and then you have a representative out of the state office that they'll send here to explain to the branch what they need to know and need to do. So it's a process. It's just not you, your own body. You don't do everything on your own because it could be wrong and could cost money. You could get yourself in trouble with your branch. So you have a guideline.

COUNTERING HATE

"I never thought of danger as much as I did that particular day."

My husband, John T., was the president of Montgomery County NAACP, and he was asked to go to Bristol, Tennessee, in 1985, by the national organization because there was going to be a Ku Klux Klan march. And when John stood up in Schaeffer Church and asked would anyone like to go with him, nobody wanted to go. And probably some of them were members of the NAACP, but they hadn't been committed to do certain things in their own county, so they hadn't been involved. Therefore, you just didn't get anyone.

I don't know whether he passed it on to the other churches or not, but it was announced that Montgomery County was to join with the people in Bristol. So we went there, and they had over one hundred or two hundred state troopers. I have never seen as many state troopers in my life, in this part of the country. They were there to protect us.

So what happened, we were in one room before the march started, and it was a funny feeling came to me, and all I could see—I'm closing my eyes now—because where I was sitting, I could see Mrs. John F. Kennedy with that pink coat dress that she had on when that shot [killed her husband]. John and all of them that were heads of the NAACP from different areas were on the podium. And it came to me if someone in here would start shooting, all I could see was her, and it kind of got me where I got nervous and then I had to get up and go out. I went to my room to get something—see it was in a hotel, getting ready to go out on the street to the march. And when I got up to my room, there was a policeman at my door. I didn't know that.

He said, "Who are you?" I told him. That's when I found out this is not as easy as I thought it might be. The national [organization] had let them know what people were going to be there, what presidents were coming and their room number from the hotel, and they had to keep anyone from going in our room. So when we did the march, you don't know who you could find, so we had that protection and didn't realize it. If I had never gone up there, [I wouldn't have known it]. But for some reason that fear came over me with this shoulder, the way I was sitting. I said, "Who could be back here," that may not appreciate what they were doing as far as being here to protect the whole city of Bristol.

But then when I came back [from our room], I gave out NAACP literature on the streets, and that's how I received that membership of the KKK. This gentleman passed by me with the memberships in his hand. And I said, "May I have one?" He handed me one and never looked at me, just kept walking. I said, "Thank you."

We had no problems. It was a lot of people. But we were there with the other Blacks to try to keep [the peace]—if anyone started anything. I never thought of danger as much as I did that particular day, and then it kind of went away. But I guess when you ask to take the fear and that away from you, you have to believe in what you pray and ask for. No use to ask for something and then you're going to not try to abide by the way you're supposed to do, and what you're supposed to ask for anyway. And when it ended up that day, I imagine from what I can remember, it was at least three to four hours with them marching.

That was about the end of wearing [the robes]. Now you don't see them with their tall hats and things, you really don't notice them in the area now. But I've noticed in the last four or five months, some areas they're beginning to want to put their tall hats on, which makes it looks more dangerous. But to be truthful, you really don't know who they are now, unless they get out and march, because they all dress in just regular clothes.

NAACP Freedom Fund Banquet

"To me, that was the most remarkable thing that could have been said for us."

We watched the chapter grow, but we watched the main issue that has been spelled out to us from the state and the national having the Freedom Fund Dinner, and we watched that grow from fifty to one hundred people, from

NAACP Freedom Fund Banquet. The Inn at Virginia Tech and Skelton Conference Center, 2019. *James Klagge.*

one hundred to two hundred, at Donaldson Brown at Virginia Tech, and now has gotten to anywhere from three hundred to four hundred, almost five hundred people. So that's something to be proud of, to know that you have to have people that are motivated and have strong leadership.

Senator [Douglas] Wilder was one of our speakers. When he got off the plane, someone went and picked him up. I don't know if John was with him. But anyway, when we got with him over at Donaldson Brown, [he reached for] his speech. He had it somewhere in this pocket—you know how men have that pocket when you open up your coat. John carried him and sat him in Donaldson Brown so when the meeting got ready to start, the ushers could escort him up to the podium.

He said, "When I got in there," he told John, "John, I've got to put this speech back in this pocket. I thought I was going to be talking to all colored people." And I don't mind it. I thought that was funny. He was in the [Virginia] Senate for twenty-five years. He said most of the Whites in the Richmond area would buy tickets but give them to Black people, and the [Whites] didn't come. And he got here—this is Southwest Virginia—we're supposed to be stupid people. You know what I mean? That's the capital down there, and you know everybody there—White and Black—they think they're above everybody else because they're at the capital. He got here, and found out he was wrong. To me, that was the most remarkable thing that could have been said for us.

How we met Senator Wilder, we were going to a meeting at the Union College in Richmond. I saw it in the paper, and I said, "John," I said, "we're going to miss this. It's going to be today." We had a wringer washer when we first came here, Maytag. And he looked at it. It was early in the morning. I said, "It's going to be this evening," whatever time it was during the day. It doesn't take but, what, about four hours, to get to Richmond. And he said, "Well." I said, "But I'm washing." He said, "That's got nothing to do with it. Unplug the machine." And we got dressed and went. As we were getting out of the car going across the lawn, this gentleman was coming up the walk. John asked him to tell him where this building was that we were going. This man said, "Well, I'm on my way there, too. I'm Senator Wilder." That's how we met him.

And from that day on, we have been more than just friends. We'd pass so many people [who'd ask], "Did your husband go to school with Senator Wilder?" I'd say, "No, you don't have to go to school to be friends with people. It's how you meet them, and how they feel about you, and what exists in that meeting, your smile, your action or your speech, or whatever you were talking about. Some things just linger with you with people. And just because he's a senator, that didn't make us have to go to school with him." So all the way down through our life, from that day on, he's been a friend.

We got tickets in advance for Lieutenant Governor Wilder to be inaugurated for governor. John got us a box. We had so many people that we didn't want to tell you to come, or maybe we did tell some, but we let it be known that we had a box seat. I said, "We've been going to inaugurations all these many years, and when they dance they would be down on the floor dancing, the Whites." We had been to three or four governor inaugurations, and we had to stand. In the case of Governor Wilder—the first Black governor in the United States—we did not.

The Table

"And [John] *said, 'I'm tired. Let's have a dinner.'"*

This wasn't connected with the NAACP, but once you're a member of something, whatever you're in, if it's good for your community, it goes with you like when you go to your church. That same thought of being good, kind to other people, it doesn't matter. It goes with you. When they started building this highway out here [late 1990s], that two-lane was leaving us, my husband said, "Nan, they tell me they're going to hire some of the colored and the low-income Whites that can't get a job at Hercules."[32] We didn't have businesses like we've got now. And he said, "I'm tired. Let's have a dinner."

Well, somebody said, "How could you all invite people to come to your house?" You know, because we don't have a good—I can't even think of the name of the furniture—type of home. And I would say, "Well, we don't look at it that way. We just look at how people share their voices and are talking to us. We just feel like they mean it, and maybe they didn't at first, but finally they saw we were going to keep coming back. I guess they said, "They don't have good sense. They're going to still keep coming."

Sweetheart, he invited the heads of the hospital, heads of the different stores. We had about twenty-some Whites to come here for dinner, and we did not have the money to do what we really wanted to do. So John said, "Well, we're going to have it, we've got to have it right." So we asked one of the Black cooks at Virginia Tech, who was a friend to a friend of ours, and we asked him. He gave us the same treatment if he had been waiting on the table for the president of the college. He had this hat on, and when he served wine, he had the towel wrapped around the wine if you wanted wine before you ate. The beef that he cooked was—I still wouldn't think I could cook it today—one half of it is done, and the other side—you know, you go in these big hotels and things. "What do you want, rare?" They ask you. They can cut it off. Then flip, roll that thing around and get the other side. I don't know how they do it, but that's what he did.

And you know how it was served? I had a coffee table. It's downstairs in the basement now. It was almost the same length as the couch. This gentleman took it and put it on top of my dining room table and made it a double deck, and when they fixed all the salads and the different things, whatever—the seafood was on there. It was so gorgeous. You thought you were at the president's house, only as far as the setting of the food and table, he charged us two dollars a plate. Can you imagine? It was cheap for us, because it should have been at least fifteen to twenty-five dollars a plate or more. But he said just to take care of the food, my charge is [negligible].

You may recall, Thompson Tire Company, they are all over Southwest Virginia now, Mr. [Joe] Thompson called another friend of ours that owned a store. He said, "I got a call." We didn't send an invitation out. We called. And he said, "What in the world do they want?" That's what he tells this other fellow, and he tells us. "Are you going?" He said, "Yes, I told them I'd be there." So Mr. Thompson said, "I'll think about it." After he called another friend and found out they said they were coming—they really came out of more curiosity than [anything]. Of course, I don't blame them. They couldn't figure [it] out. John said, "Just to wine and dine, and then you'll hear the rest when you get here." And that's how we got them.

But he was trying to get some relationships with people and let them know that we are a part of the community, and you just don't keep telling us like you do a child. Tell you one thing, and then you find another story to tell me the next day, because you're not going to buy me the wagon I want. And that's how we created a conversation between people and businesspeople here in the community, and it just grew.

It's been a good relationship with us with the Caucasian families and with businesspeople. My husband was a person, if you had a business and you fired someone, and he came to you and asked you, and sometimes it has been White, because low-income Whites have problems just as bad as we did, and still do. He'd come back to you the second time, maybe you have all these houses for low-income people and they're not paying the rent like they should. You know, the town pays so much and whoever, whatever area, and they pay the rest, and they're not paying their part, and you're going to put them out. And when they called my husband and he goes and investigates, they always had somebody on the committee with him.

A lot of people would ask, "Well, what is Mr. Hairston doing?" You never hear of things that get done so well. The only reason that I think John got as much done back then without having a lot of confusion is he would say to you, "Now, I'm going to give you until tomorrow to make up your mind what you're going to do. If not, I'm going to have to take it to the newspaper." And that would make you come across with some kind of answer that made us feel that you're going to do, and you probably will have it done before the week's gone, or within time limit, to keep any problems in that area from happening. I try to tell people now, "You've got to have a way of knowing how to address yourself to people to get something done."

Chapter 6

LEGACY

"That is my motto: To make this a better world, let it begin with me."

A Life with the World

When John and Nannie Hairston moved to Virginia in 1953, they built a good life for their family and helped build a better community for the town of Christiansburg, Montgomery County, the state of Virginia and, in fact, the nation. Nannie told me many times that her parents taught her "wherever you move to, be a part of your community." Indeed, she did.

She and John joined Schaeffer Memorial Baptist Church (where they were long-standing deacon and deaconess), the PTA, the local branch of the NAACP and the Democratic Party. They volunteered. John joined St. John's Masonic Lodge No. 35 and the American Legion Post 182 and led the nonprofits Christiansburg Housing Corporation and the Health Systems Agency of Southwest Virginia. Nannie was a founding member of the League of Women Voters of Montgomery County, joined the New River Valley Historical Society and the St. John Chapter 80 Eastern Star and served on local boards such as for the United Way. She was a member until her retirement of the Political Action Committee of the Local No. 3-495 Oil, Chemical and Atomic Workers International Union.

The local NAACP branch particularly benefited from their volunteer efforts. They were both lifetime members and were among a small group of members operating in the 1950s when the branch had a small membership and kept it alive with their actions and funds. John served as president from 1983 to 1989. Nannie held various branch executive positions, including treasurer, served as membership chair for more than twenty years and helped organize the local Youth Council. In addition, she served on the Virginia State Conference Board of Directors.

They had a special place in their hearts for Schaeffer Memorial Baptist Church, Schaeffer Community Cemetery (where they are both buried) and the Christiansburg Community Center. The Center at various times housed a Community Action Program, Christiansburg Head Start, a clothing bank, a senior center, a tutoring program and a program for Black history. The Hairstons were involved with numerous renovations at the Center. They served on the board continuously until their deaths and kept the organization afloat with their own funds. The Christiansburg Community Center continued to be one of Nannie's major fundraising efforts until her death in 2017.

The Hairstons were also very involved in their community in non-organizational and non-institutional ways. They temporarily housed African American students from Virginia Tech when they were prevented from living on the campus. They counseled many young African Americans and helped them find employment in the area. And they assisted low wage-earning Blacks and Whites who needed help with their rent or with their landlords. Their good works also included helping some young people financially with their college educations. They were role models and leaders.

John Hairston was invited to the Kennedy Center in 1972 to be named one of America's outstanding volunteers by the National Center for Voluntary Action. Nannie Hairston was invited to the White House in 1980 by President Jimmy Carter to attend a reception for Robert Mugabe, prime minister of Zimbabwe, the realization of a dream she had as a young girl growing up in the coal fields of West Virginia.

Nannie Hairston was the recipient of many awards in her lifetime, including "Mother of the Year" by Schaeffer Memorial Baptist Church in 1986, an award that held special meaning for her. Other awards included "Citizen of the Year" from Omega Psi Phi Fraternity, 1986; Virginia Women of Distinction Award from Virginia State Conference, NAACP, 1997; Maggie L. Walker Community Service Award from Virginia Conference, NAACP, 1997; the Christiansburg Rotary Club award for Community Service; induction into the West Virginia All Black Schools Sports & Academic Hall of Fame in 2008; and the Dominion Energy and the Library of Virginia's Strong Men and Women in Virginia History award in 2013.

Daphne Maxwell-
Reid and Nannie
Hairston, Virginia
State Conference,
NAACP, and the
Virginia Legislative
Black Caucus. "A
Tribute to Women
of Distinction,"
Richmond, Virginia,
September 13, 1997.
Hairston family.

One award requires special mention. She was the first recipient of the Nannie B. Hairston Community Service Award in 1991 by the Montgomery County–Radford City–Floyd County Branch (7092) of the NAACP in "recognition of her most dedicated and distinguished service to her community." The award is presented annually to a member of the branch who has shown outstanding public service. There have been more than thirty recipients of this award to date, and the awardees have included university presidents and professors, civil rights and community activists, reverends and ministers, women and men, Blacks and Whites.

She was particularly proud to have played a part in having a bronze sculpture of Captain Charles S. Schaeffer created and installed at the Schaeffer Memorial Baptist Church in 1997. Her own bronze sculpture grew out of her relationship with sculptor Larry Bechtel, who was the sculptor for the Schaeffer bust, and it is installed in the Montgomery County Government Center. An unveiling and dedication celebration was held on October 28, 2006, at the Center along with a resolution by the Town of Christiansburg to "commend Mrs. Nannie Berger Hairston for promoting kinship and serving to remind us all that each of us can make a difference in the world." It is fitting that a physical representation of Nannie Hairston will stand in the government seat of the county that she became such a part of and in which she made such a difference.

In 2011, Christiansburg mayor Richard Ballengee declared June 14, John's birthday and their wedding anniversary, John T. and Nannie B. Hairston Day. After her death in 2017, the Virginia House passed Joint Resolution no.

Left: NAACP Freedom Fund Banquet. Nannie Hairston and Raymond L. Bishop, winner of the Nannie B. Hairston Service Award, 2015. *James Klagge.*

Opposite: Colette Hairston Hash with her grandchildren (Justus, Vivian, Farrar, Trè, Drae and Harper). *Colette Hairston Hash.*

134 "Celebrating the life of Nannie Mae Berger Hairston" in January 2018. John had also been given a resolution after his death (House Joint Resolution no. 837). Last but not least is the John T. and Nannie B. Hairston Endowed Scholarship Fund at New River Community College, a fund that Nannie started in 2013 with the funds she received from Virginia's Strong Men and Women Award.

Nannie Berger Hairston's legacy, importantly, includes her daughters, sons-in-law and grandchildren. She was very proud of her family and spoke of them often with love and respect. They were close. In going through her archive, I found many deeply meaningful cards, letters and artwork from her children and grandchildren that she saved over the years. She told me that she was doing the oral history for her grandchildren and great-grandchildren so that they could know their own history.

But she also frequently spoke of the needs and values of all children and the need to teach the younger generation love, kindness and responsibility. In her acceptance speech for the 2013 Strong Men and Women Award, she said, "I want children to remember that the most important part of your life

is your character. It goes with you all through your life. I learned long ago that to make it a better world, it had to begin with me." Her life stands as a testament to this statement, and her legacy will go beyond her children and her grandchildren to the children (and adults) who learn about this icon of civil rights and her life with the world.

FAMILY

"I did this [oral history] *mostly for my grandchildren
and my great-grandchildren."*

My father, Samuel Berger, was born in 1893 and expired 1978. He was born in Franklin County, Virginia, on October 8, 1893. My mother, Bessie Mae Robinson Berger, was born in 1903, and expired in 2008. She was born in Burnt Chimney, Virginia, on May 8, 1903. I want to say: I did this [oral history] mostly for my grandchildren and my great-grandchildren. Then if they ever have to know who their great-grandmother was—my father's mother, Annie Mariah Berger, and my grandfather was Peyton Berger.

My mother's mother died when my mother was eight years old. My father's mother and father died before he was sixteen years old. So I only had one grandparent growing up in my life—there were ten children in the family—and actually, after me, none of the children had grandparents, because my mother's father died when I was eleven years old.

I have to tell this. I never had an opportunity to visit my parents like the average young men and women who say, "I'm going home for the summer. I'm going home for Christmas." I only lived three miles from my parents, and when I left Amonate, we brought my parents here with us. So I never was away from my parents, which I thought was great. I lived around them all my life.

I was blessed with a babysitter and parents, too. I would think about it, when the girls would come in from different cities, some grandchildren coming in from Des Moines and coming from overseas where they stayed, I never had that opportunity because I was always with them. I tell my baby girl [Colette Hairston Hash] now that lives in Pulaski, I say, "They always say what goes around comes around. I used to take care of your children. Now you're picking up your grandchildren from school." My mother did the same for me, so it's been handed down.

It's nice when you look back over your life and can see the things that your parents taught you and you were able to teach your children, and you can see it in your grandchildren. When we were growing up, the things that children say to their parents—we weren't allowed to even dream of it

Bessie and Samuel Berger. *Hairston family.*

or think of it almost, and now children say it because the parents allow it. But I grew up in an atmosphere where you just didn't say things like that, and I tried to pass it on to my children, and it worked very well. I have four daughters, and sometimes they say you're tooting your own horn, but I thank God that I had the privilege of having parents, that the foundation I got from them, it really worked for me for my children and I've seen it work for their children. So it's nothing new. It's just that people don't get that background and that's why the world is like it is.

We have been fortunate to have had a lovely life. Sometimes I say we went too far with our children, but they seem to still love us. I used to tell my husband, after we began to get where we were slowing down, I'd say, "You know, it's a wonder our children love us as much." We didn't do anything that would make them feel like we were abandoning them. But I felt like sometimes, maybe we should have been at home more. We were out volunteering a lot, but then we came back home. We had a busy schedule.

We asked ourselves questions—even after we had children, the first two girls [Catherine and Edwina]. They grew up with us. We told them, "If you see something that we're doing you don't like, you come and tell us, and we'll sit down and talk about it as parents, because there's some things that we may be doing that can hinder your life." We did that with our four girls. Our four girls have had that handed down to them, and in talking to some of my children, sometimes they tell me what their children are telling them, and they say, "Mother, when you really think about it, we have had a beautiful life with the things that love has handed down."

Mr. Brad Stipes is one of the town councilpersons. He asked me if he could come here and talk to me. He'll be back in town in two weeks. But I'm saying that to say this: He said, "I went to your husband's funeral. I have been to a lot of funerals, but to hear the grandchildren speak about him [was impressive]. And when the last grandchild spoke at John's funeral, it was my youngest granddaughter, who had just graduated from law school. She said, "Granddaddy set the bar high for us, and we need to remember this."

Hill School/Christiansburg Community Center

"God blessed us to be able to help other parts of our community."

I suppose the reason I got involved with the Christiansburg Community Center, which was [known as] Hill School, the first [Christiansburg] Industrial Institute, was when I found out that it was given to Schaeffer Church when Captain Schaeffer came here and started it. First he started it in a log cabin. We talk about integration and racism and all of this going on in the country [today]. But just think, that church was built by the Freedmen's Bureau sending Captain Schaeffer here to be the managing person to erect these buildings just after the Civil War. When I talk to people, I say, "You know, we've been integrated ever since the 1800s."

A few weeks after I was here, I joined Schaeffer Memorial Baptist Church. After four or five months, within a year, John and I found out some things that we felt we could work with if we wanted to do volunteer work in the community. The [Schaeffer Community] Cemetery was one, which Captain Schaeffer gave for [former] slaves to be buried. That's the way it's written. He left it not to Schaeffer Memorial Baptist Church, but he asked that the deacons and trustees of Schaeffer Church see that it would be kept up. And when John and I first came here, it was very weedy, trees growing around it, and some of the people that were interested in it were trying to get it clean or brush cut around certain graves and things. So then he and I began to take interest in the cemetery before we did the Community Center. And we found out Mr. S.H. Clark, a gentleman that I've talked about mostly from the NAACP, felt very strongly about trying to do something with the cemetery to keep it in shape when we have funerals.

But coming back to Schaeffer, we could see the need to have some things that we could be of help as doing missionary work or volunteer work towards the church. Ronnie Caldwell was the person that refinished the wooden pews at Schaeffer. After bringing them from the church in Philadelphia in 1866, nothing had been done with them. The Women Workers Club took it on themselves to raise the money to help pay for the renovation of our church. Mrs. Rosa [Thomas] Holmes and Mrs. Belle Mae Thomas and myself were the committee to bring ideas to the group to get money to fund this project. And then I think I have mentioned to you we had no furnace or no air conditioning. The church had been brought up to par before we learned that we could enter into the national and the state register as a historical building. I do feel that my husband and I were a part of something that happened good for the community.

The next thing that we got involved in was the [Christiansburg] Community Center. I don't know exactly how we got so involved in it, because Mr. S.B. Morgan and Mrs. Rosalie Paige were having some kind of classes in the Center. Right now, it won't come to me the name of the organization that they were working with. But we didn't have a floor in the bottom, just like the dirt floor. See, they would heat it with coal, the furnace. It was heated with coal, and whenever they bring the coal for the stoves for the school, they shoot it through a window down into the basement.

But in the meantime, my husband saw what was happening there, then he decided that something needed to be done with his time after the doctor made it clear with him that he wouldn't be able to work anymore at public [places]. So then that's when he decided, when he was talking with his son-in-law, James McDaniel, my oldest daughter's [Catherine's] husband, and he made a statement, "Daddy John, there's a lot of money floating in Washington."

So he decided, not right off the bat, but in the next week or month or so to organize an organization. He put it in the newspaper. Anyone if in the first five or seven—you know, usually when you want to have something like that, you have either three, five or seven, so when you organize it has to be odd numbers. If something is tied, you have someone to vote it up or down.

If you have a committee of seven or five people, six people vote for it, tied it, then you've got to have the odd person. So the first seven people that came and gave him money, which was he said $100 apiece, and he would organize. It would take that amount of money to go to Richmond, have everything drawn up to be legal. So we didn't have any Caucasian people to come, and it ended up with these Black [people]. It was two women and the rest were men, and some were from Schaeffer Church and some were from Asbury Methodist Church. [A few names: Kenneth B. Wright, Mrs. Geneva McDaniel and Walter Price.]

[The Christiansburg Housing Corporation] was organized, then they put in for monies. And from there, they started building houses, and then they had money. Then they created a thing that, there's a gentleman here in this community, in this county, named George Dalley. He came here to set up a Community Action Program. And no one in the area would tell him about a building, especially Caucasian churches. He hadn't found anywhere. So wherever he ran across John, I don't know how that happened. So Mr. Dalley came to Schaeffer Church. Some people felt like before it was voted on, to let him start doing this. Some thought maybe the government was just going to come in and take our property. Well, you can understand how people felt back then, and some would feel that way now if you hadn't been oriented in knowing how things work. So Mr. George Dalley came to the church, and they authorized. So then we got enough money, and I can remember the money that was given to operate a daycare center: $220,000. But anyway, in order for us to have a daycare there, you had to have a basement. That's how we really got involved with the basement going in.

Our pastor at that time was Reverend Kenneth Wright. He worked with him just like the other volunteers, digging that basement out to put a concrete floor in it so we could do the other part to have Christiansburg Community Center, a daycare. My husband said to me, "I go down and look at it and tell them we're going to have to dig some more." A couple of young people would ask him, "Well, why do we have to keep on digging, Mr. Hairston?" He said, "Whenever I come down here, we've got to have so many inches of concrete poured. If we don't dig enough down, then I'm going to have to stoop over when I come down." My husband was six feet, five and a half inches tall. And he said, "We're going to have to dig so when we put the concrete, I can walk around here standing straight up."

So they achieved that, and then we received the money. For years, we had a clothing bank. We started housing the clothing bank upstairs in the Community Center, and we had that to offer for in-kind to the community.

Then Schaeffer Memorial Baptist Church, up until today, they have always paid the water bill and the light bill. That's what they contribute towards the Christiansburg Community Center for their contribution in-kind. From then on, we just worked and it has been a building that—that's why we're so interested and want to have it fixed now. We have nowhere [else].

I don't know how to say it. It doesn't sound real, what I'm getting ready to say. We served continuously with the CCC board. We have never stopped working for the Center from the day we started, regardless who was on the board. If we could do anything, we were always adding somebody else on the board to do the Center. If something needed to be done and some people felt like, well, we just don't have faith that it can still be done and keep the building open. I've known a time when we didn't have money to buy oil. Mr. [Howard] Bane, who owns the oil and coal company here, John would call and ask him to go and fill up the tank of oil, and we charged it to ourselves to keep the Center open.

But I'm saying that [to show] how graceful God has been to us to have in our minds, to do things for the community. We couldn't afford it in a sense, but God blessed us to be able to have people to help us by letting us have credit, and we'd charge it to our own account. Maybe that's the reason we didn't have as much as we should have in our bank account, but God blessed us to be able to help other parts of our community.

Nannie Hairston at the Christiansburg Community Center, September 1, 1999. *Hairston family*.

CAPTAIN SCHAEFFER BUST

"I just felt like maybe there were tasks that God had planned in my life to do certain things, and that was one of them."

Mr. Larry Bechtel was told by a young lady who was the president of Christiansburg Industrial Institute Alumni that he should come and ask John Hairston and his wife to take him to Schaeffer Church to see Captain Schaeffer's picture. So he did, and we carried him. That was my first time knowing Mr. Larry Bechtel. And when he got to the organ, he looked at the picture and he said, "Oh!" I thought something happened to him. I said, "Something wrong, sir?" He said, "No. I thought [Captain Schaeffer] was Black." And that has really been something to me when he said that, because whatever he had read, he still hadn't seen a book of him or a picture of him. He just thought he was a Black person.

Mr. Bechtel and his wife—his wife's name is Ann—are really extended family friends. We became friends through Captain Schaeffer's sculpture, and then when he did the sculpture, he said he was going to give it to John and me for the church. I looked at it and I said, "Well, what are we going to do with it?" It wasn't bronze. It just had pink cheeks and it looked like him. I said, "Well, why can't we have it in bronze?" He said, "You realize how much money it would cost?" And I did, not the amount, but I realized it was going to cost something.

So Mr. [Robert] Freis was a news reporter for the *Roanoke Times*. And he said, "Do you want me to put the article in the paper?" I said, "If you will." And that's how we got started. I have things in this book [scrapbook], I think, where some people wrote and said it's long overdue of Captain Schaeffer being recognized of doing what he did for Afro-Americans.

I have a picture of Roselawn [Memorial Gardens] cemetery where the director [Terry Welch] gave the granite base that the sculpture is on. She told me, "It probably will cost you no less than $2,000 wholesale. I would let you have it." But when she found out what it really cost, she gave it to me for the Captain Schaeffer [sculpture]. Wasn't that something?

And that was how things happened. Just different people, with the article in the paper, started sending money. And then I asked my pastor, Pastor [Lee E.] Suggs, could the treasurer receive the money and not put it with the money of Schaeffer Church. But he could receive it and keep it, because no way in the world I could keep up with it. We didn't have a committee. I just

Above: Larry Bechtel and Nannie
Berger Hairston. *Hairston family*.

Right: Captain Charles Schaeffer bust,
2023. *Josh Rosenfeld*.

felt like maybe that's my task that God had planned in my life to do certain things, and that was one of them.

Mrs. Rosalie Franklin Paige wrote, and she started out, "We've been friends since the '50s," and this was in 1997 when she wrote the letter. She said, "I know Captain Schaeffer's wife, Mrs. Ada Schaeffer, would be happy to know that a woman came to Christiansburg from West Virginia and took this project and had her husband's sculpture done." If I hadn't found that letter, I wouldn't have known that she wrote this.

NANNIE MAE BERGER HAIRSTON BUST

"You know, it's almost unbelievable."

Mr. Bechtel and his wife became friends, and then when he wanted to enter into a contest in Washington, D.C., to one of the new places that I just noticed where they're raising funds for, some church gave a million dollars. Some Black church gave a million dollars in the Black paper to this place in Washington. I really don't know the address or anything about it, but I do recall him coming to me. He asked his wife, said, "I would like to enter that contest and see if I win, it would be in that building. Who would you pick? And I'm not going to tell you who I have already in mind." Then she said, "Why wouldn't you do Nannie?" And that's how it came about that he did my sculpture.

Then after he did it, he didn't know where to put it after he didn't win. He went to the museum here. I don't know if you've been to it. But anyway, he felt like it should be somewhere where there's more traffic. There was nothing wrong with the place, but it wasn't enough traffic, he felt like. I did a joke with him, or at least I felt like it was a joke and he laughed about it. I said, "Well, Mr. Bechtel, since you can't find anywhere to put it, why don't you try the Highway Department in Richmond, and maybe they'll let you put it out here on IH 81." He laughed. So after that, he came up with the idea to go to the county supervisor [board], which is seven people, and they had to vote on it.

My daughter asked me the night they were going to vote on it, "Mother, do you want to go?" I said, "No." Really, the reason I didn't want to go, I didn't want them to feel like I'm here, maybe that might make you want to vote for it. So I told them, "No, I don't care to go, and if they vote it down, I still love everybody. And if they vote it up, I still love everybody." So that's what happened. She called me and said, "Mother, it passed. They're going to put it in the [Montgomery County] Government Center." It's just a small

Hairston family at Nannie Berger Hairston's bust unveiling at the Montgomery County Government Center, October 28, 2006. *Hairston family.*

thing to have happen, but it's a great thing to know that you live in a county of eighty-some-thousand people, and Afro-Americans are less than four thousand people. You know, it's almost unbelievable.

It shows what can happen in a community, how things have changed from one generation to the next generation, because when we came here I know it wouldn't have happened like it did, because I know the attitude that we found out how some people were in the county. And the county, I have seen a turnover of the way we have been treated, down from one supervisor and mayors and different people that we have come in contact with down through the years. We have never had problems with any one. Just to say a problem, I can't pick out one. But I've seen a lot of changes.

COMMUNITY

"No race left behind."

I'm just thinking how we have gone through so much, because our family back in 1619 came here from Africa. We got here before the people from Europe got here, 1620 to 1621. We were already here, and we tilled the soil, built America, and we still—it's almost like you hear the president say, "No child left behind." I say, "No race left behind." We're still trying to pull ourselves up with our bootstraps to make us to be what we want to be as citizens in America.

But what I'm saying, when you think about it, what people went through—You didn't have to go to Alabama and Georgia and Mississippi. Right here in Montgomery County, just like New York or any other place. And you had to look at people and think, "What a blessing, how God can work through people," and how some of us have gone through such hardship and then still not hate. That's the beauty part of all of it.

We were just ordinary people. But somehow or other our relationship [with Virginia state senator Madison Marye, for one], with whatever way we had it, going to Democratic meetings and met him, and we have been friends all the way down to now. I have read a letter since I've been talking with you back and forth, getting in my books and reading letters coming from senators and different people that if you would tell some people, they wouldn't hardly want to believe it until you show it to them. But that's just the way our life has been.

I'm trying to say, I really want young people [to know], if you don't go to college, you can have good relationships with people without going to college, and doing for your community. You don't have to go, because a lot of us send our children to college. When I say a lot of us, we have children going, but if they haven't been taught the beauty of looking behind, don't leave like we see people, you know they're behind you. Are you helping them to try to get them to go forward? And if you don't try, you have a community of people and wonder why they're like they are, they have nobody to think of them.

I feel that we've done just what we felt like we could do, and it's nice that people recognize us as well as they have. But I have felt all along that you do what you can do, and the next person does what they can do, and it comes together. But I had no idea in life that we would be recognized as doing some things that maybe would not have been done if God hadn't placed it in our hearts and minds to do it.

When people come to my home and they look at the plaques and they'll ask me, "How do you get them?" But we didn't ask for them. It just automatically has been given to us. The community felt that we should have a plaque for doing what we have done in the community. It's a blessing now, since I got where I can't get out. When people ask me how do you get them, well, you have to do things in the community. You may not do what I have been doing, but it's always so nice to do it and do it with love and kindness and a peaceful mind. And that's one thing that I can always say about what my parents taught us: If you're going to do something for someone, try to do it out of love and kindness.

John T. and Nannie B. Hairston
Endowed Scholarship Fund

"We had…a life with the world."

Well, I look at my life now since I've gotten older, and Miss June Sayers, since I became a friend of hers. I never dreamed of even helping someone with a foundation and never dreamed of myself of having a foundation [the John T. and Nannie B. Hairston Endowed Scholarship Fund at New River Community College]. But we have always given, and when I say helping, the highest that I have ever known for us to give one student at one time was $500, and it was a person right here in Montgomery County. This young man said he couldn't go back to college because he didn't have enough money to go back for a second semester. So John said, "Well, Sugar, I think we could do that, couldn't we?"

I'm just saying, down through the years, relatives and friends and school activities and things that have been going on in the community, we feel that that was just as important of helping someone else as it was sending my own children to college, right here in Montgomery County, not only away from home. I mean, when I say away from home, in another area, like West Virginia where I came from, if we knew of someone who needed help and someone brought it to our attention, if we were able, we did it. That's just been my life.

What I'm trying to say, it takes all of us, if we have something that we can offer to our community. That is my motto: "To make this a better world, let it begin with me." And I think I try to show that. My husband tried to show that. And we didn't try to show it as a thing to make other people feel that they weren't doing anything, but that's just our part that we felt like we could share in the community, and I think it has rubbed off on a lot of people.

The most important thing I can say, I have four daughters, and I'm proud to speak these words: All four of my girls, wherever they are, and their husbands, they have the same attitude towards their community, regardless of the race, color or whatever. If they can do something, it rubbed off. It

Nannie Hairston and her daughters. *From left to right*: Edwina, Colette, Catherine and Dy-Anne, on the occasion of her granddaughter Erica Penn's graduation from the College of William and Mary Law School, May 2014. *Hairston family*.

Nannie B. Hairston, seated in the first row at President Barack Obama's campaign appearance in Roanoke, Virginia, July 2012. *Steven Cochran*.

John and Nannie Hairston, 2011. *Hairston family.*

may not sound like good English to say it rubbed off, but I can see what my parents taught me, it was in me. My husband's parents taught him, and it was there, and it was two people ever since we started out in life. Whatever was wrong, we tried to right it. I think that was the reason we were able to live and have a good marriage and raise four children, have four lovely sons-in-law after seventy years of marriage.

But we had so many other people in our life. And talking with you—sometimes I say, "Why would they want to write a book about it?" Then I go to my books and read the cards and things that people are thanking us, and never tell you what they're thanking you for but something we had said or done. I realize we had—not just with our four girls and my parents—a life with the world.

Afterword

HOW I CAME TO TELL
NANNIE BERGER HAIRSTON'S STORY

A native and lifelong Texan, I moved to Virginia in 2010 in my mid-fifties to marry for the second time. My new husband was an emeritus English professor from East Carolina University who decided to retire to the Blue Ridge Mountains of Virginia. I was in the mood to take a chance in my life's third act—my son was in graduate school in California—and so I moved from Austin, Texas, where I had lived for more than thirty-five years, to the village of Floyd, Virginia.

I was fortunate to find work almost immediately with the History Associates Inc. out of Washington, D.C. I subcontracted with this organization to conduct oral histories with retiring university president John Casteen and three of his top administrators from the University of Virginia in Charlottesville, about 150 miles from my new home, during 2011–12. My next project was closer to home. The Historical Society of Western Virginia hired me in 2013 to conduct oral histories with retired employees for the Norfolk and Western Railway and current employees for Norfolk Southern, in Roanoke, which is about forty miles from Floyd. I wrote the book *African American Railroad Workers of Roanoke: Oral Histories of the Norfolk & Western* (The History Press) on a tight deadline, and within the year, it was published, in June 2014.

Doty Elizabeth-Oliver Smith, a local salon owner (in Christiansburg), and my stylist and friend, as well as Mrs. Hairston's stylist and friend, gave Mrs. Hairston a copy of my book—proving once again the power inherent in beauty shops and women supporting and networking with one another. After Mrs. Hairston read my book, she enlisted her friend June Sayers, who was the business manager at the Montgomery-Floyd Regional Library in Christiansburg, to contact me. I did indeed meet with June at the Library in the summer of 2014 and then wrote a proposal to conduct a life history with Mrs. Hairston.

I met with Mrs. Hairston in December 2014, and we agreed to work together on the project. The Montgomery-Floyd Regional Library hired me. During the course of the spring of 2015, I wrote a proposal to the Virginia Foundation for the Humanities, which had been one of the funders of my railroad book, and the grant was approved in June 2015. June Sayers wrote grant proposals to the Community Foundation of the New River Valley, the Montgomery County Friends of the Library and the Montgomery-Floyd Regional Library Foundation, and those grants were awarded.

Mrs. Hairston and I met over a six-month period, from August 2015 to January 2016, for a total of sixteen sessions and twenty interview hours. In doing the background research for the grant writing and for the project during the spring of 2015, I was awed by the number and prestige of the awards she had received and her notoriety and place in the community. So, when early on in our meetings she referred to herself as a "non-professional woman without an advanced degree living in a small town," I responded that she couldn't fool me—she was much more powerful than that and had been an important and integral part of our American story. Indeed, in our time together she proved that to me time and again.

When I met Mrs. Hairston, she was an icon in the community, one of the power brokers of the Democratic Party in Virginia, a leader in the NAACP and highly revered by the community at large. As a newcomer to Virginia, not having a place in the community through employment or membership in an institution, society, club or organization, and being much younger than she, about the age of her youngest daughters, I had every reason to be in awe. However, we did share some important things that gave us common ground: We were both mothers, both held middle-class values, both were political liberals (I believe), both loved history and both enjoyed fashion. Most importantly, we were both highly invested in and committed to the project at hand: Mrs. Hairston telling her story for posterity.

We treated each other with kindness and respect. She often mentioned my quiet patience (an important skill for an oral historian). And she tirelessly explained to me in detail how things had worked in her life through all the different phases as one might explain to a younger newcomer who did not totally understand the intricate processes and procedures of her life's history. And there was a lot to explain. Although I had done my research, I didn't know much about coal mining or coal mining communities, traditional religion, women's clubs and voluntary associations, not to mention the embodied experience of being African American growing up during Jim Crow with its racist laws and societal segregation and degradation, nor being on the front lines of the civil rights movement in order to change that discriminatory system.

I was born in mid-twentieth-century Texas and raised by a divorced mother of three daughters. I was close to an extended family of grandparents, cousins, aunts and uncles who lived in a rural part of the state, although my mother ended up in Houston, where I graduated from high school. I then paid my way to the University of Texas at Austin in the mid-1970s. I received my undergraduate degree in cultural anthropology in 1977. I came of age during the "New History" era, when the study of history was influenced by the social movements of the 1960s and 1970s. The new framework called for history to be told from the "bottom up" and to include ordinary Americans— those who had been left out of the history books—and to look through the lens of race, gender, class and ethnicity. And, importantly, it included new or newly appreciated methodologies like oral history. I began my oral history work as an undergraduate with an honors thesis, "The Traditional Woman's Role in a Small Texas Town." I had always been an empathetic listener drawn especially to the stories of my grandmothers, but I also received a rigorous training in the art and science of oral history at the university.

I went on to graduate school in the American Studies Department at the University of Texas and later worked at the (now) Briscoe Center for American History, where I learned more about the field. I have conducted more than four hundred oral history interviews in my thirty-some-odd-year career with award-winning judges and lawyers, civil rights activists, astronauts, scientists and artists, among many others. But my primary interest has always been bringing to light the stories of those who have been forgotten or neglected or willfully expunged from history. The underlying promise of Mrs. Hairston's and my work together was that in telling her powerful story of resilience and telling how she and her family overcame the odds stacked against them might be a hopeful tale for future generations and for all of us as we continually try to perfect our union and become closer to the ideals our country was founded on.

Our interview sessions were chronologically based but open-ended. My interview questions included subjects such as her childhood, family background, education, recreation, mentors, siblings, communities in which she lived, instances of racism, the effects of Jim Crow, World War II, the Korean War, the Civil Rights Act, integration, childbirth, employment, the civil rights movement, her involvement in organizations including the NAACP and the Democratic Party, voting, her children's education, the church's role in her life, her involvement with Christiansburg Institute and the Hill School and friends, as well as the community at large. In telling her own story, she, of course, told her husband John Hairston's story, as their lives were entwined for more than seventy years, and the story of her family and children. The sessions were held at her home in Christiansburg and were usually one hour in length. We met when she was ninety-four years old, but her memory was sharp, and she interspersed her stories with photographs or documents that she pulled from her many scrapbooks that she kept to document her life. She would say things like, "I do have some pictures to prove some of the things I've been telling you. I think it makes it nice whether you're writing a book or if you're telling a story." (October 7, 2015)

Oral history, of course, is the remembrances of individuals, and memories do not always adhere to strict historical facts. Memories actually offer a more important function—that of creating meaning from life experiences for the narrator and adding important details and perspectives to historical narratives that may have been excluded from the dominant story. I have made every effort to ground Mrs. Hairston's oral history in historical detail by using newspapers, other oral histories, journal articles and scholarly books, among other sources. In some cases, I've used the information found in the very scrapbooks that Mrs. Hairston kept. I take full responsibility for any dates, facts, misspelled names or other inaccuracies that may be found in the book.

Our sessions were professionally transcribed, and I then edited them for accuracy and readability while being careful to preserve her meaning. Usually, at this juncture in an oral history project, I would print the transcripts and ask the interviewee to review them or, more frequently these days, I would send digital copies that the interviewee edits using track changes. However, in this case, due to Mrs. Hairston's age, I decided to read the transcripts aloud to her and annotate them with her additions, deletions and edits as we went along. This was the first time in my career that I had done that. It was a long process—there were a total of seven hundred pages.

We finished our editing sessions at the end of 2016, and I then made her corrections and changes to the transcript. She signed the release form for the Montgomery-Floyd Regional Library Foundation on March 9, 2017. It was an interesting process for me—the experience of conducting the interviews in the first place, and then re-experiencing them in telling them to her, heightened the power of the stories and their poignancy. And Mrs. Hairston agreed, saying on January 21, 2016:

> *I can't explain to you what this has meant, that I didn't feel that what we were doing—and people were sending cards to us, and we were thanking them, but I had no idea that all of this was going to come after. But since it has, then I go back over when you leave or I go to bed at night, and it's almost like visiting someone. You're visiting your own life.*

Beyond our professional relationship, I believe, we developed a friendship. She often spoke about the importance of having friends of all ages and from all walks of life. It was hard not to like, respect and admire Nannie Hairston. We discussed many topics outside of our scheduled interviews, and she was more than conversant in current events.

During the time we were meeting, racist incidents occurred at Christiansburg High School involving the Confederate flag. In September 2015, twenty students were suspended for wearing clothing with the Confederate flag because it was against the Montgomery County School District dress code. The students were purportedly protesting the new rule as of the school year 2015–16 that students who wished to park their cars in the school lot could not display the Confederate flag. This incident received national news.[33] She spoke about concerns she had for her grandchildren.

Mrs. Hairston was very aware of the backlash happening in the country that seemed to be a reaction to the election of Barack Obama as the first African American U.S. president. She did not believe that we were living in a post-racial society. But as the previous pages attest, Mrs. Hairston was not an angry person. In fact, I have never met someone who lived her life in such a loving way toward all others. Nannie Hairston is an example of what writer and historian Rebecca Solnit has said: "Most great activists—from Ida B. Wells to Dolores Huerta to Harvey Milk to Bill McKibben—are motivated by love, first of all. If they are angry, they are angry at what harms the people and phenomena they love, but their urges are primarily protective, not vengeful. Love is essential."[34] Mrs. Hairston lived her life in accordance with Christian principles, following Jesus's instruction to "Love your neighbor as yourself." Like Martin Luther King Jr., she believed that "Darkness cannot drive out darkness, only light can do that. Hate cannot drive out hate, only love can do that," and more importantly, she acted on that belief.[35]

She was not afraid to confront injustice, but she did so with compassion. It seems to me that the recent work of activist and professor Loretta J. Ross has followed in Nannie Hairston's footsteps. Ms. Ross has a new book coming out early next year, *Calling In: How to Start Making Change with Those You'd Rather Cancel.* She said this in a *New York Times* article about her work in 2020: "We have a saying in the movement: Some people you can work with and some people you can work around. But the thing that I want to emphasize is that the calling-in practice means you always keep a seat at the table for them if they come back."[36]

Nannie Hairston died on July 14, 2017. It was devastating for her family, of course, for the community and for me. Although she was ninety-five—and very close to her ninety-sixth birthday—her death felt untimely because she was so full of life to the end. Some of the terms that were used to describe her at the time, at the funeral service and in the media, included "Queenly," "Freedom Fighter," "Civil Rights Icon" and my own, "Missionary of Love and Social Justice."[37]

I remember that one of the speakers at her service suggested that it may take some time and distance to be able to adequately appreciate her legacy. Well, it did take a few years from the end of processing our oral history interviews in 2016 for me to get her book to the publisher. Those years for me held a move, other contracts and projects, the COVID-19 pandemic and some unavoidable delays in the researching and writing process. Working on this book over the last months and listening again to her words has led me back to what feels like her powerful presence.

In choosing the book's interview excerpts that comprise the chapters, I've been guided in part by her suggestions at the time, by stories that are especially powerful or poignant and by stories that are particularly descriptive of an era, subject, individual or event, or stories that tell more about who she was. I have removed my questions. The chapters are arranged in chronological order. I have written an introduction and a preface for each chapter that places it in historical, cultural and at times geographical context. My hope is that her words are as powerful to the reader as they were and are to me.

As I am completing the manuscript in June 2024, it has not been lost on me that the country has been living through significant anniversaries in the struggle for civil rights, which are so much a part of her story and our American story: the seventieth anniversary of *Brown v. Board of Education*, the sixtieth anniversary of Freedom Summer and the sixtieth anniversary of the Civil Rights Act. Last year marked the sixtieth anniversary of the March on Washington, and next year will mark the sixtieth anniversary of the Voting

Rights Act. The years between 1954 and 1965 have been called the "heroic age of the civil rights movement."[38] The period has come to be symbolized by Martin Luther King Jr. and a few other high-profile leaders. However, there were many local community activists and leaders, parents, church members and others who were instrumental in the struggle. It is my hope that this book, in telling the story of one such African American woman in a small southern town, joins important scholarship that has been done to broaden our understanding of this crucial period in our American story.

It was one of the great honors of my life to listen to and record Mrs. Hairston's life story, to be a co-creator, if you will, in the oral history interview sessions that I conducted with her over that six-month period. Mrs. Hairston spoke to me about "the book," her book, many times and always saw it as a result of our interviews. She would often say, "I don't know if you'll want to put it in the book or not," or "I wish you would use this photograph in the book."

It is an even greater honor for me now to have completed this book—that, yes, I crafted by choosing the excerpts, arranging them, writing the context for and choosing which photographs to include, but in the majority of these pages, Mrs. Hairston tells her own story. So, from my perspective, the book was written with a "shared authority," a concept in the field of oral history that has come to mean how the process and product of oral history can have a shared authorship.[39] To that end, and to honor our joint authorship, any proceeds I receive from the sales of the book will be shared with the John T. and Nannie B. Hairston Endowed Scholarship Fund at New River Community College.

Finally, then, I have fulfilled my promise to her—ten years after our first meeting—and am sharing with the world the remarkable life of Nannie Berger Hairston, in her own words, so that people can learn about her accomplishments, her dignity, her grace and her wisdom. This is Nannie Hairston's personal story—a life filled with love, heartache, achievements, difficulties, happy moments and tragedy as is true in any life. But as she was an African American woman living in the South who came of age during the middle of the twentieth century, the story also includes the challenges of living under the racist restrictions of Jim Crow and the valiant struggle for equal rights. It is my hope that her story shows that the struggle for equality and social justice was a battle fought on many fronts, not just in Greensboro or Washington, D.C., or Selma, but also in Southwest Virginia and by a woman who believed in the power of love.

NOTES

Introduction

1. Population figures for West Virginia found at "West Virginia Archives and History," West Virginia Department of Arts, Culture & History, accessed June 25, 2024, https://archive.wvculture.org/history/teacherresources/censuspopulationrace.html.
2. Robert Wood Johnson Foundation, "2020 West Virginia Report," accessed December 27, 2020, https://www.healthdata.org/sites/default/files/files/county_profiles/US/2015/County_Report_McDowell_County_West_Virginia.pdf.
3. Corbin, *Life, Work, and Rebellion in the Coal Fields*, 5.
4. Ibid., 10.
5. Trotter, *Coal, Class, and Color*, 69.
6. David A. Corbin, "The Mine Wars," West Virginia Encyclopedia, March 1, 2023, accessed June 25, 2024, https://www.wvencyclopedia.org/articles/1799.
7. Abby Lee Hood, "What Made the Battle of Blair Mountain the Largest Labor Uprising in History," *Smithsonian Magazine* (August 25, 2021), accessed August 16, 2022, https://www.smithsonianmag.com/history/battle-blair-mountain-largest-labor-uprising-american-history-180978520.
8. Chris Williamson, "Black Miners and the Battle of Blair Mountain," *U.S. Department of Labor*, blog, accessed June 25, 2024, https://blog.dol.gov/2024/02/22/black-miners-and-the-battle-of-blair-mountain.

9. Archives at Tuskegee Institute, "Lynchings: By State and Race, 1882–1968."

10. Valk and Brown, *Living with Jim Crow*, 8.

11. Lisa McMillion, "True Colors," *Register-Herald*, April 20, 2011.

12. Brendan Wolfe, "Lynching in Virginia," Encyclopedia Virginia, Virginia Humanities, December 7, 2020, https://encyclopediavirginia.org/entries/lynching-in-virginia.

13. Archives at Tuskegee Institute, "Lynchings: By State and Race, 1882–1968."

14. *Roanoke Times*, "William 'Morris' Phillips Obituary," August 25, 2009.

15. *Roanoke Times*, "Large Number Pupils Listed in Montgomery," August 27, 1953.

16. Wallenstein, *Virginia Tech, Land Grant University*, 192–93.

Chapter 1

17. Most likely Mrs. Hairston is referring to L. Roncaglione, "Personal Notes," *Coal Age* 39, no. 1 (1934). "L. Roncaglione, for 4½ years a mine inspector for the Pocahontas Corporation, has been appointed superintendent of Nos. 30, 31 and 32 mines of the company, Amonate, Va."

18. Mercer County Convention & Visitors Bureau, "The Millionaires Tour," last updated April 29, 2019, https://visitmercercounty.com/itinerary/the-millionaires-tour.

Chapter 3

19. Dan Thorp, e-mail to author, February 21, 2023.

20. Kanode, *Christiansburg, Virginia*, 93; Architecture of *The Negro Travelers' Green Book*, "Eureka Hotel," University of Virginia, last modified November 10, 2023, http://community.village.virginia.edu/greenbooks/content/eureka-hotel.

21. My research has suggested that Mrs. Hairston was referring to the Bell Capozzi House Bed & Breakfast, 201 East Main Street, Christiansburg, Virginia, 24073, now a private residence again.

Chapter 4

22. Schaeffer organized more than twenty African American churches in the nearby counties of Pulaski, Giles, Wythe, Campbell, Pittsylvania, Floyd and Botetourt. Kanode, *Christiansburg, Virginia*, 63.
23. Virginia Landmarks Register Online, "Old Christiansburg Industrial Institute," Virginia Department of Historic Resources, last updated February 19, 2024, https://www.dhr.virginia.gov/historic-registers/154-5004.
24. Robert Freis, "A Day to Remember," *Roanoke Times*, March 2, 1996.
25. National Center for Voluntary Action, "Christiansburg Man Cited as One of the Nation's Top Volunteers," press release, February 10, 1972.
26. Kanode, *Christiansburg, Virginia*, 63.
27. Charles H. Harrison, *The Story of a Consecrated Life: Commemorative of Rev. Charles S. Schaeffer, Brevet-Captain, U.S.V.* (Philadelphia, PA: Lippincott Company, 1900).
28. My research has suggested that Mrs. Hairston was referring to Joan Hardie Munford, and the restaurant was Hardie House.

Chapter 5

29. Interview with author, January 13, 2023.
30. Montgomery-Floyd Regional Library, "The Life and Legacy of Nannie B. Hairston," YouTube, August 11, 2018, https://www.youtube.com/watch?v=X6ODAyH3LZA.
31. Nick Rush public comments, "The Life and Legacy of Nannie B. Hairston," August 11, 2018.
32. Elissa Milenky, "Bypass Project Gets Final OK," *Roanoke Times*, July 19, 1996.

Afterword

33. Daniella Silva, "Virginia Students Suspended After Protesting Confederate Flag Ban," NBC News online, September 17, 2015, https://www.nbcnews.com/storyline/confederate-flag-furor/christiansburg-virginia-students-suspended-after-wearing-confederate-flags-disrupting-school-n429456.

34. Rebecca Solnit, *Whose Story Is This?: Old Conflicts, New Chapters* (Chicago: Haymarket Books, 2019), 112.

35. On the south wall of the Martin Luther King Jr. Memorial in Washington, D.C., quotation from his book *Strength to Love*, 1963, National Park Service, last updated June 11, 2024, https://www.nps.gov/mlkm/learn/quotations.htm.

36. Jessica Bennett, "What If Instead of Calling People Out, We Called Them In," *New York Times*, November 19, 2020, updated February 24, 2021.

37. Sheree Scarborough, "Nannie B. Hairston: A Missionary of Love and Social Justice," *Roanoke Times*, August 6, 2017.

38. Joseph, "Reconceptualizing the Heroic Period of the Civil Rights Movement, 1954–1965," 6.

39. Michael Frisch, *A Shared Authority: Essays on the Craft and Meaning of Oral and Public History* (Albany: State University of New York Press, 1990).

SELECTED BIBLIOGRAPHY

Catte, Elizabeth. *What You Are Getting Wrong About Appalachia*. Cleveland, OH: Belt Publishing, 2018.

Chafe, William H., Raymond Givens and Robert Korstad. *Remembering Jim Crow: African Americans Tell About Life in the Segregated South*. New York: New Press, 2001.

Cline, David, Amy Starecheski and Brooke Blackmon Bryan. Review of the book *A Shared Authority: Essays on the Craft and Meaning of Oral and Public History* by Michael Frisch. *Oral History Review* 44, no. 2 (2017): 372–82.

Corbin, David Alan. *Life, Work, and Rebellion in the Coal Fields: The Southern West Virginia Miners, 1880–1922*. Champaign: University of Illinois Press, 1981.

Frisch, Michael. *A Shared Authority: Essays on the Craft and Meaning of Oral and Public History*. Albany: State University of New York Press, 1990.

Gates, Henry Louis, Jr. *The Black Church: This Is Our Story, This Is Our Song*. New York: Penguin Press, 2021.

Gill, Tiffany M. *Beauty Shop Politics: African American Women's Activism in the Beauty Industry*. Champaign: University of Illinois Press, 2010.

Gordon, Linda. *The Second Coming of the KKK: The Ku Klux Klan of the 1920s and the American Political Tradition*. New York: Liveright Publishing Corporation, 2017.

Green, Kristen. *Something Must Be Done About Prince Edward County: A Family, a Virginia Town, a Civil Rights Battle*. New York: HarperCollins Publishers, 2015.

Hannah-Jones, Nikole. *The 1619 Project*. New York: New York Times Company, 2021.

Harrison, Charles H. *The Story of a Consecrated Life: Commemorative of Rev. Charles S. Schaeffer, Brevet-Captain, U.S.V.* Philadelphia, PA: J.P. Lippincott Company, 1900.

Joseph, Peniel E. "Reconceptualizing the Heroic Period of the Civil Rights Movement, 1954–1965." *Souls* (Spring 2000): 6–17.

Kanefield, Teri. *The Girl from the Tar Paper School: Barbara Rose Johns and the Advent of the Civil Rights Movement.* New York: Abrams Books, 2014.

Kanode, Roy Wyete. *Christiansburg, Virginia: Small Town America at Its Finest.* Kingsport, TN: Inove Graphics, 2005.

Lindon, Mary Elizabeth. *Virginia's Montgomery County.* Christiansburg, VA: Montgomery Museum and Lewis Miller Regional Art Center, 2009.

Morrell, Gene. *Heroes Among Us: World War II Veterans of Montgomery County and Radford, Virginia.* Charlotte, NC: Jostens, 2007.

Norkunas, Martha. "The Vulnerable Listener." In *Oral History Off the Record: Toward an Ethnography of Practice.* Edited by Anna Sheftel and Stacey Zembrzycki. London: Palgrave Macmillan, 2013.

Painter, Nell Irvin. *The History of White People.* New York: W.W. Norton & Company, 2010.

Solnit, Rebecca. *Whose Story Is This?: Old Conflicts, New Chapters.* Chicago: Haymarket Books, 2019.

Thorp, Daniel B. *Facing Freedom: An African American Community in Virginia from Reconstruction to Jim Crow.* Charlottesville: University of Virginia Press, 2017.

———. *In the True Blue's Wake: Slavery and Freedom Among the Families of Smithfield Plantation.* Charlottesville: University of Virginia Press, 2022.

Trotter, Joe William, Jr. *Coal, Class, and Color: Blacks in Southern West Virginia, 1915–32.* Champaign: University of Illinois Press, 1990.

Valk, Annie, and Leslie Brown. *Living with Jim Crow: African American Women and Memories of the Segregated South.* London: Palgrave Macmillan, 2010.

Wallenstein, Peter. *Cradle of America: A History of Virginia.* Lawrence: University Press of Kansas, 2014.

———. *Virginia Tech, Land Grant University, 1872–1997: History of a School, a State, a Nation.* Blacksburg: Virginia Tech Publishing, 2021.

Werner-Thomas, Holly. "Is Oral History White? The Civil Rights Movement in Baltimore, an Oral History Project from 1976, and Best Practices Today." *Oral History Review* 49, no. 2 (2022): 377–98.

Wilkerson, Isabel. *The Warmth of Other Suns: The Epic Story of America's Great Migration.* New York: Random House, 2010.

INDEX

ABOUT THE AUTHOR

Sheree Scarborough is an oral historian with more than thirty years of experience co-creating oral histories and directing oral history projects. She is the author of *African American Railroad Workers of Roanoke: Oral Histories of the Norfolk & Western*, based on her interviews with railroad workers. She holds an MA and is ABD in American Studies from the University of Texas at Austin, where she was an oral historian for the Briscoe Center for American History. She also directed the Frank Erwin Oral History Project, documenting the life of the former chairman of the Board of Regents at UT. She has worked as an oral historian for the Library of Congress, the National Institutes of Health, NASA/Johnson Space Center, the University of Virginia, the Historical Society of Western Virginia and the National Museum of Women in the Arts.